Live The[atre]

Six Plays from the North East

The Filleting Machine, You Are My Heart's Delight, Shooting the Legend, Wittgenstein on Tyne, Laughter When We're Dead, Cold Calling

Tom Hadaway was born in 1923 in North Shields and began writing at the encouragement of C. P. Taylor. Most of his stage plays were premiered by Live Theatre, including *Seafarers*, *The Long Line* and *God Bless Thee, Jackie Maddison*. He has also worked with the North-Eastern film company Amber Films and the BBC has broadcast eight of his television plays.

C. P. Taylor was born in Glasgow in 1929 but lived in Northumberland for the last twenty years of his life and was closely associated with Live Theatre. Over thirty years he wrote prolifically for both the theatre and television. He wrote *And a Nightingale Sang* (1977) for Live Theatre and *Good* (1981) for the RSC. He died in Newcastle in 1981.

Alan Plater became a full-time writer in 1961. His first radio plays included the Sony Award-winning *The Journal of Vasilije Bogdanovic* (1983) and his work for television began with contributions to the pioneering *Z Cars* series; more recently he wrote the screenplay to the much-acclaimed *Last of the Blonde Bombshells* (2000). His prolific work in the theatre includes *Close the Coalhouse Door* (written with Alex Glasgow and Sid Chaplin) and *Peggy For You* (Hampstead Theatre and West End, 1999) as well as more recently *The Last Days of Empire* (Watermill Theatre, 2003). Other plays for Live Theatre include *In Blackberry Time* (with Michael Chaplin), *Going Home*, and *Tales from the Backyard*.

Lee Hall was born in Newcastle-upon-Tyne and studied English Literature at Cambridge University. His other stage plays for Live Theatre include *Cooking with Elvis*, *Bollocks*, and *Two's Company*. He has written extensively for radio, including *I Love You, Jimmy Spud* (Sony Award, 1996) and *Spoonface Steinberg* which was filmed for BBC2. His adaptations include Brecht's *Mr Puntila and His Man Matti* and *Mother Courage and Her Children*; *A Servant to Two Masters* (from Goldoni), and Heijermans' *The Good Hope* (National Theatre, 2001). His screenplay for *Billy Elliott* (2000) was nominated for an Oscar. Two volumes of his plays are published by Methuen.

Sean O'Brien is a poet, critic, playwright, broadcaster, anthologist and editor. He is Professor of Poetry at Sheffield Hallam University, is poetry critic for *the Sunday Times*, as well as being a contributor to the *Times Literary Supplement* and the *Guardian*. He has written five collections of poetry and has twice won the Forward Prize for Poetry. His verse version of Aristophanes' *The Birds* was staged at the National Theatre in 2002 and his new play *Keepers of the Flame* premiered at Live Theatre in November 2003.

Julia Darling was writer-in-residence at Live Theatre from 2000–02. She has had a long relationship with the theatre and written projects such as the Tyneside Mystery Cycle and *NE*1. Her radio plays include *The Black Path* (with Sean O'Brien) and *Sea Life*, her fiction includes *Taxi Driver's Daughter*, and her poetry includes *Sudden Collapses in Public Places*.

LIVE THEATRE

Six plays from the North East

The Filleting Machine by Tom Hadaway
You Are My Heart's Delight by C. P. Taylor
Shooting the Legend by Alan Plater
Wittgenstein on Tyne by Lee Hall
Laughter When We're Dead by Sean O'Brien
Cold Calling by Julia Darling

Introduced by Lee Hall

Edited by Max Roberts

Methuen Drama

METHUEN CONTEMPORARY DRAMATISTS

Published by Methuen 2003

1 3 5 7 9 10 8 6 4 2

First published in 2003 by
Methuen Publishing Limited,
215 Vauxhall Bridge Road,
London SW1V 1EJ

Methuen Publishing Limited Reg. No. 3543167

A CIP catalogue record for this book is available from the British Library.

ISBN 0 413 77409 0

Typeset by SX Composing DTP, Rayleigh, Essex
Printed and bound in Great Britain by
Cox and Wyman Ltd, Reading, Berkshire

Caution

This anthology is financially assisted
by the Arts Council of England

Contents

Preface   vii

Introduction   xi

The Filleting Machine   1

You Are My Heart's Delight   27

Shooting the Legend   49

Wittgenstein on Tyne   139

Laughter When We're Dead   159

Cold Calling   257

Preface

The year 2003 sees the thirtieth anniversary of Live Theatre
Company, Newcastle-upon-Tyne. Founded by Geoff
Gilham and Val McLane, the company began life touring
its devised work to social clubs, pubs, community centres
and schools, reaching audiences who might not normally
choose to visit established or conventional theatres. The
material was political in content and strong in regional
identity and was performed by actors whose vernacular
delivery spoke directly to their audience.

Tom Hadaway first became involved with Live Theatre
around 1974 through his association with director Murray
Martin and Amber Films, who had taken the company
under their wing. Tom's defining play *The Filleting Machine*
was instrumental in achieving initial revenue funding for the
company from Northern Arts (now Arts Council North
East), which has remained a principal stakeholder and has
supported this volume. Impeccably constructed, *The Filleting
Machine* marked the beginning of a long-term creative
relationship with Tom. Over fifteen of his plays have since
been commissioned and produced by Live Theatre. This
relationship was also the genesis of Live's new-writing policy
– which has remained integral to the company's work
throughout the thirty years of its existence.

Tom's mentor was Cecil Philip Taylor, a prodigiously
talented Glaswegian Jewish writer who had settled in the
North East. He too was soon to form a strong link with the
company, initially through director Paul Chamberlain, who
directed the premiere of *A Nightingale Sang in Eldon Square* –
another landmark production in the company's history.
Cecil was not only a prolific writer for the theatre but also
played a significant role in shaping the dynamic artistic and
literary scene that was fast developing in the North East
during the late 1970s and early 80s. By the time of his tragic

and untimely death in 1981, aged 51, he had become one of the leading writers of his generation, and Live Theatre had produced over fifteen of his plays. Teddy Kiendl, who was Director of Live in the late 70s and early 80s, enjoyed a fruitful partnership with both Cecil and Tom, and his work saw Live establish itself as one of the country's foremost small-scale touring theatre companies. Live Theatre's venue is now dedicated to C. P. Taylor's memory.

Alan Plater began his long-term association with Live Theatre during the 1980s; he has had seven plays produced to date by the company. *Shooting the Legend* was also the first co-production between Live and Newcastle's Theatre Royal, a development necessitated by Alan's enormous local popularity and his unique ability to amalgamate his distinctive humour and wry observation with a natural affinity for his Tyneside audience.

The mid 1980s found the company halfway through the loving but painstaking development of its premises in a complex of ancient warehouses and almshouses on Tyneside's historic Quayside. Live's home now houses a unique 200-seat cabaret-style theatre, offices, rehearsal space, bars and a café.

Having worked with Cecil, Tom and Alan, I was fortunate enough to witness the emergence of an exciting younger generation of Tyneside writers in the 1990s, including Lee Hall (author of, among others, the play *Cooking with Elvis*, and the screenplay *Billy Elliot*), Peter Straughan (*Bones, Noir*) and Julia Darling. The work of these writers has done much to raise the company's profile nationally and has figured prominently in the cultural development of the Northern region, gaining an international profile in recent times and having a significant impact on Tyneside's economic and social regeneration. Live has been in the vanguard of this movement and a visit to Tyneside today should include a walk along the Quayside where the venue plays an important and increasingly expanding role in Gateshead and Newcastle's rapidly developing cultural quarter.

Live Theatre houses the largest free arts participation

programme in the city, run by Live Lines, the company's
education, training and outreach department. Live's youth
theatre provision serves over 200 young people aged
between eleven and twenty-five, with weekly sessions being
held both in the theatre and in the community at satellite
youth theatres in the east and west of the city. The
department also manages Live Wires, a writing and
performance group for the over-50s. There are several
opportunities for all of these groups to perform on Live's
stage and on tour throughout the year. Live Theatre also
hosts an extensive yearly programme of New Writing
Development events including workshops, a script-reading
service, rehearsed readings and lectures for new writers.

From 2001 to 2003, Julia Darling and Sean O'Brien were
jointly Writers-in-Residence at Live. Sean, one of the
country's leading poets (he is the only poet to have won the
Forward Prize twice), and Julia, a novelist and poet, winner
of the Northern Rock Foundation Award (the largest literary
award in the UK), used the residency to embrace and
expand their dramatic writing, allowing both writers, in
common with Live, to broaden their opportunities and
potential audience. Sean's first play, *Laughter When We're Dead*
was performed at Live in June 2000; his most recent play for
the company, *Keepers of the Flame,* a co-commission with The
Royal Shakespeare Company, premiered during their
annual residency in Newcastle in 2003. Julia's *Cold Calling,*
the final piece in this volume, began as a stage play and was
adapted for the screen in a co-production by Live for Tyne
Tees and Yorkshire Television.

Each play in this anthology has a brief introductory note,
which tries to contextualise the play. Early archive
information is, however, somewhat vague, so the notes are
from memory and received anecdote. There is, of course, a
host of other writers whose work could have been included
here – Leonard Barras, Phil Woods, Michael Wilcox, Steve
Chambers, Peter Flannery, Michael Chaplin, Karin Young,
and Gez Casey, to name only a few.

I hope this volume will serve as an acknowledgement of
the work of a company that has resolutely striven to serve its

audience, providing a platform for the North East's finest writing and acting talent over three decades. It is to all these people that the book is dedicated.

I've asked a proper writer to pen an introduction. It seemed appropriate, especially when that writer, Lee Hall, saw first-hand some of the company's early work while he was a pupil at Benfield High in Newcastle's east end, a regular venue on Live's early tours.

Max Roberts
July 2003

Note

For more information about Live Theatre please contact:
27 Broad Chare
Quayside
Newcastle-upon-Tyne
NE1 3DQ

www.live.org.uk
info@live.org.uk

Introduction

Live Theatre currently occupies a two hundred-year-old bonded warehouse on Newcastle's quayside. Opposite is the resplendent law court with its armed guards, and across the beautiful Millennium Bridge, which sits virtually outside the door, is the Baltic Centre and the vast mushroom of the new Sage Music Centre. The view now, compared to when I first ventured down to the quayside about twenty-five years ago, is unrecognisable. Where the new cultural centre is were working warehouses, a mile or so of ramshackle tin sheds storing God knows what shipped in from down the oil slick of a river. It was all rusting, down-at-heel and foreboding, very obviously a place of work, even though it looked in some kind of decay. Now, however, the river is purely for recreation. A place to slake a thirst and contemplate the breathtaking transformation.

The plays in this volume tell the story of that transformation. I grew up in a region steeped in the culture brought about by the Industrial Revolution. This was a town where physical strength was at a premium. Life was hard and so were the people. They were rightly proud of their skills and hard labour, and although impoverished in terms of their wealth they were rich in spirit. In relative terms the men were better paid than the women which gave them an independence from the matriarchy which ruled the roost at home. The archetypal Geordie worked hard and played hard, was robust, good-humoured and fiercely independent.

As I grew up in Newcastle in the 1970s this culture seemed immutable. You could see the shipyard cranes from my bedroom window which was several miles away. There were local factories on the way to school. It seemed this was the way things were and would always be. What none of us really understood was this was its twilight. It is no secret that the 1980s were extremely bleak years for Britain's industrial regions. An economic and cultural attack on the very basis of their existence was waged by central government and exacerbated by the phenomenon we now know as globalisation.

Suffice to say all the certainties vanished. All the tired clichés of provincial working-class life started to vanish at an alarming rate. The shipyards closed, mining collapsed. The steel works vanished, vast tracts of what was once the most vibrant part of the city (and is ironically again) – the riverside – became virtually derelict. Eventually, unemployment was followed by the influx of call centres and other such parasites of the service economy, but a vast new underclass, disenfranchised and despondent, was left in the wake. All the skills once thought essential to survive in the harsh northern climate were at worst redundant, at best in need of complete rethinking.

Along with the dwindling of heavy industry went the demise of the social institutions which had been a mainstay of life in the North for a hundred years. The local Co-ops became Kwiksaves, theme pubs overtook working-men's clubs as the hub of entertainment, and the unions simply dwindled. But at the same time other groups became powerful. Women's roles changed enormously, as they found their skills had more economic valency in this brave new world. The ethnic make-up of the city changed dramatically. This change in the underlying fabric of economic existence presented massive challenges in the way people related to each other The traditional hierarchies in familes, in work, in the very language that we all used, were challenged. Lives were in transition and a new culture was overtaking the old.

But now even, as this process has come to the end of its first phase and the 'city of culture' has overtaken the city of work, the emotional legacy of the old world still lives on. This new landscape of leisure and art is itself a place where versions of culture are contested. An emblematic moment for the region was the dressing of Antony Gormley's *Angel of the North* in a Toon Army shirt. The irreverent spirit of

Tyneside was not buried with the factories that forged it. Culture on Tyneside is something live, something to criticise, appropriate and to find pride in.

Anyway, as in countless cities the world over, the artists sniffed out development opportunities long before the developers. Live Theatre, which had started as a peripatetic troupe that took theatre to the people, made a derelict building their home and were way ahead of the developers, and indeed Heseltine and Thatcher whose masterplan of regeneration is fundamentally responsible for the shape of the rebirth of the riverside.

Because Live Theatre was a base for new writing, because it was forged in the spirit of addressing local people about the way we live today, because they took theatre to the places where people congregated, the theatre and the plays it commissioned had a different feel from those one could see at the other theatres in the region. Their new venue on the quayside was more reminiscent of a club or a cabaret than a theatre. You sat at table and could drink, smoke and chat. Even now, although the stage is the focus of the room, the space is dominated by the audience. There are no neat rows, there is no proscenium to hide behind, no them and us. Instead, there is a democracy of people in one room. So all these plays were written with that audience very much at the heart of their concerns.

This is very different from much writing practice in this country, where many new plays are addressed to the theatre community, to other playwrights, to critics, to metropolitan taste, or indeed simply to the playwrights themselves. All of which are entirely legitimate pursuits , of course. But the plays at Live were always about trying to communicate to the community directly around them. In this way a lot of the early writing has much in common with the best of TV writing. The poetry of the demotic, the absurdity of the everyday and the music of the cornershop were all useful tools to represent the world as we knew it. It is no coincidence that Tom Hadaway and C. P. Taylor were successful writers for TV at the same time as they were forging an identity for Live.

The kind of work they made laid a certain foundation for all the plays to come. The combination of the irreverent, the pathetic, the wryness towards political cant while being thoroughly informed by a socialist perspective were qualities shared by almost all the plays produced at Live. They are unafraid to be emotional or poetic, but are also funny and robust. If they represent pathos the sentimentality is always undercut with a salty sense of humour. Tom Hadaway's beautiful miniature completely captures the signal moment of change which runs through the whole collection, where new labour challenges the old. This time without the capital letters, but the ground of the entire political gear change are set out in this one-act piece. The final image of the young girl who would rather listen to music broadcast in from afar rather than make her own seems to haunt the entire collection. It is especially poignant in a play which so brilliantly finds music in the speech of ordinary people.

The later plays in the volume are all informed by the same basic way of looking at the world, and looking at drama. Even though Sean O'Brien's prodigious first play is a political drama in verse it still bears all the hallmarks of an unspoken Live tradition. It is lively, ribald and fun in equal measure to tits anger and seriousness. Set on the Quayside of the future it presents New Labour with the return of everything it has been repressing. Alan Plater's contribution is a very funny piece in the well-made-play tradition, perfectly constructed, but absolutely on top of all the ironies about trying to represent the new reality while still living partly in the past. As different to each other as each of these plays are, they are absolutely connected by the examination of an economy and, therefore, whole lives in transition.

Although my own contribution is set in the past, it was very deliberately trying to tackle the same theme: the confrontation of the parochial with the forces which threaten its very existence. In a culture which defines itself by what it excludes, the question of sexuality is both a metaphor and also a real theme which has obsessed Live writers. C. P. Taylor's play, my own and Julia Darling's piece all examine the prejudice and loneliness faced by people whose sexuality is not endoresed by the place and time in which they are living.

C. P. Taylor's play shows that the coming of the new economic realities were not simply the preserve of industrial Tyneside and examines the effects of new ways of living in the coutnryside. Again, it is a play with much to say about culture, in this case recorded music, and is self-conciously tackling the nostalgia that attends any moment of change. Julia Darling's play is about selling one's self, among many other things, and finds in its examination of sexuality a way of talking about the much larger forces that are shaping this particular moment of transition. But again it is by turns funny, sad and quietly radical, and again is an example of Live's links with television as it was broadcast by Tyne Tees.

The delightful thing about working at Live is it has no pretensions. Each of these plays modestly tackles its subject matter, but when you put all these pieces together I think they present a panorama on which you can read a narrative in which a whole society is moving from one place to another. They are witness to this transition but are by no means neutral. They declare themselves desperate, I think, to cling on to the advances of the past which are in danger of being swept sway in the process of change.

But at the same time these plays are unafraid of the liberties we are allowed as the stranglehold of past prejudices loosens. Sometimes, it was easly living in the North-East during this period, to feel one was in the midst of a vast stagnation, and that we were writing about stasis, and were frustrated by the slow pace of change – but, in retrospect, reading these plays, perhaps the reverse was true and it was a period of immense change. I suppose, as writers we have been blessed by living in interesting times, even if the plays we've left behind are littered with it victims.

Lee Hall
September 2003

The Filleting Machine

Tom Hadaway

The Filleting Machine was first performed by Live Theatre Company in the Central Club, North Shields, in 1974, with the following cast:

Alice	Annie Orwin
Davy	Sammy Johnson
Ma	Val McLane
Da	Tom Hadaway

Directed by Murray Martin

As part of the company's thirtieth birthday celebrations, the play was revived at the Live Theatre, on 11 March 2003, with the following cast:

Alice	Stephanie Lacey
Davy	Adam Scott
Ma	Denise Welch
Da	Trevor Fox

Directed by Max Roberts
Designed by Imogen Cloet

Author's Note

Born on Waterville Road, North Shields and schooled at
'Ralphies' on the Ridges Estate, I left at 14 to end up on the
fish quay. There I met pal and fellow fish filleter 'Muts' who
would say wise/funny things like '"There's two sorts of
education! Sort the' keep for thorsel's an' the sort the' give
to us"'. He could boast it took six polis's to bang him up,
and he had the bruises to show, but a machine arrived that
could cut fish faster than ten men, and this giant of a man
was undermined. *The Filleting Machine* is his story, and of a
Ridges family struggling against the odds, written before
that estate's change of name to the Meadowell, and a
quarter of a century before its riots brought ill famed
prominence. Intellectuals told me 'it demonstrates the
intrusion of economic forces into the lives of ordinary
people'. I'd never thought of that, I just loved Muts, Ridges
people and C. P. Taylor who advised me, 'write from your
own back yard'.

Editor's Note

During the initial rehearsals of this play in 1974, the actor
playing the part of Da became 'indisposed', and so for the
first performance Tom played the part himself (script in
hand but never referred to, apparently). So successful was
the evening that he went on to repeat the performance over
a hundred times throughout the region, from Berwick to
Middlesborough and from South Shields to Barrow.

Characters

Ma, *in her fifties*
Da, *also in his fifties*
Davy, *their eldest son*
Alice, *their eldest daughter*

Scene: A council house living room, with kitchen.

Offstage: The house is on the Ridges estate, North Shields. The area is a depressed enclave of poor whites who have been slum-cleared from the fish-dock district. In the distance, the raucous strident sound of children in the battlefield of the street can be heard.

Ma *is preparing a meal.* **Alice** *calls from offstage.*

Alice   Mother! Mother!

Ma   Hellow!

The door opens and **Alice** *comes bursting in.*

Alice   The bairn's covered wi' baked beans, an' tea leaves.

Ma   Gawd almighty!

Alice   Tattie peelin's, an allsorts reet in the pram.

Ma   That dorty buggar upstairs. Tossin' his rubbish oot the winder.

Alice   It's all claggy. Yuk! (*She limps across the room. One of her legs is bandaged.*)

Ma   Tryin' ti get the dinner on. An' look at the state o' that bandage. Fresh on this mornin'. Ye'll end up with it septic.

Alice   Better take a flannel, the pram's *lathered.*

Ma *snatches a cloth from a drying line.*

Ma   Take that buggar a piece o' me mind. (*She leaves and we hear her voice offstage, receding.*) Ye great lazy good for nowt. Ye've got the place covered wi' yor filth.

Alice *switches on her transistor radio. Music. She wanders over to the window to listen to the altercation outside.*

Ma   Aye! Thor's none so deef as doesn't want ti hear. Fancy hevin' ti live under dorty buggars like you.

Alice *wanders back to a chair, sits and takes up a comic.*

Ma   Ye want bloody sortin' out.

The kitchen door opens and **Davy** *comes cautiously in. He is dressed in a wind jacket and rubber boots.*

Alice   Hi, Davy!

Davy   What's up?

Alice   Upstairs! Covered the little'n wi' shit.

Davy   Oh!

He begins to take off his jacket. **Alice** *studies him.*

Alice   Where you been?

Davy   Doon by.

Alice   On the fish quay?

Davy   So what?

Alice   Get yor hammers if she finds out. Better hide them wellies.

Davy *considers confiding a secret. He stands up holding his boots.*

Davy   Gotta job.

Alice   Gotta what?

Davy   Gotta job.

Alice   On the fish quay?

Davy   Start o' Monday.

Alice   Ye haven't?

Davy   Wanna bet?

Alice   Ee! what ye ganna tell Ma?

Davy (*doubtful*)   Jus' tell her.

Alice   She'll gan crackers.

Davy   Who cares?

Alice   She'll lose her blob.

Davy (*irritated*)   Alreet! Alreet!

Alice   What aboot yor interview for the Town Clerk's?

Davy (*contemptuous*)   Oh! that! That's had it.

Alice   Eee! She'll gan daft.

Offstage, **Ma** *can be heard returning.*

Ma   Bloody wasters.

Alice   She's comin'!

Ma   Neither work nor want.

At the sound of his mother, **Davy** *panics, grabs his jacket and boots and prepares to bolt into the kitchen.*

Davy   Now you shut yor gob, Alice, or A'll shut it for ye.

Alice   Push off.

Davy *retreats into the kitchen.* **Alice** *turns up the radio and a second later* **Ma** *comes in through the main door.*

Ma   A dunno. He'll put nowt in that bin. 'Cept a Friday when he's passin' it on the way ti the social security. Ye bugs. Likes o' them pickin' up a ticket. Alice! Torn that blarin' thing off. (*She switches the radio off.*) One row after another. (*From the kitchen comes the sound of a tap running. She looks in the direction of the sound.*) Is there somebody out there? Davy? Davy? Is that you, son? (*She pauses, then shouts.*) Davy!

Davy   Aye, Ma!

Davy *comes in. He pushes past his mother, snatches the comic from his sister and sits.*

Ma   Come on, bonny lad, it's past five o'clock. (*She sniffs enquiringly in the air.*) Yor da wi' ye?

Davy   No, Ma.

Ma   S'funny, could've sworn A smelled him.

Davy   Gotta lock-in. Doon at Charlie's.

Ma (*outraged*)   Gotta what? Has he had you in the boozer?

Davy   Aw, Ma! A'm owny fifteen.

Ma   An yor a big fifteen, an' yor da's a big idiot. Now come on, A want the truth.

Davy   Jus' seen him gannin' in with his mates. Ye knaa! Chopper, Sainty, Danny Mac. Charlie gi' them a lock-in.

Ma   Mates! Bloody wasters more like it. Dissolvin' thor brains wi' broon ale. Three-card brag 'til yon time. They'll take him ti the cleaners. Another short week. (*Suspiciously, she sniffs again. She comes directly over to* **Davy** *and bends over him.*) Poo! It's you. It's you, isn't it? Ye smell like a gut barrel. No wonder A thought yor father was in the house.

Davy   Aw, ma.

Ma   Ye've been doon on that quay, haven't ye?

Davy   Ma!

Ma   Now come on. A want no lies.

Davy   Just gi' me da a hand ti wash a few boxes oot. Gettim a quick finish.

Ma   A'll finish him.

Davy   Bob Wilson give's a quid.

Ma   Nivvor mind aboot Bob Wilson. Ye'll get the smell o' fish on ye. Gans right thro' yor claes, into yor skin, an' thor's no gettin' rid of it.

Davy   Ma!

Ma   Now, Davy, A've telled ye.

She goes to the mantelpiece to take a letter from an ornament. While her back is turned **Alice** *gestures to* **Davy** *urging him to tell* **Ma** *about the job.* **Davy** *summons up his courage.*

Davy   Ma! When A was on the quay . . .

Ma   Now look, son, forget about the quay. Ye've got that interview next week. (*She demonstrates the letter.*) This is your chance in life. Ye've got yor O levels, Davy, it's yor chance ti mix wi better people.

Davy   What's better aboot them?

Ma   Well, maybe thor no better than us, son, but thor not on casual. They've got positions. Davy, it's yor place on the bus. Don't end up like yor da.

Davy   Nowt wrong wi' me da.

Ma   Nowt wrong wi' donkeys, but the' divven let them on busses.

Davy   Sooner hev me da, than any o' them in the Toon Clerk's. All paper hankies for snot rags.

Ma   Davy! Divven be si coarse.

Davy   Ma, hev ye seen them? Stuck in thor desks. No proper winders ti look out. All that frosty glass, like the' hev in bogs. Pathetic! Sittin' pretendin' ti be doin' summick important. All the time, starin' sideways, ti see who's comin, an' gannin', wishin' it was thorselves. Might as well be at skule.

Ma   School, Davy. School, not skule.

Davy   All right! School, skule, what's the difference?

Ma   A'll tell ye what the difference is. It's when the' go home at night. Thor not comin' ti the Ridges estate. No, they're livin' where flowers has the chance o' growin', an' a young laddie like you isn't just summick the polis has ti keep an eye on. Where ye can hev respect, an' yor own front door, an nee female welfare supervisor demandin' to be in, ti cut yor pride off at the knees. Aye, by God, that's the dif'rence. (*Pause. She moves across to the window to glance out.*) Aye, an' when the' hang thor washin' oot in the mornin', it's still there at dinner time.

Davy   Ma, yor a patter merchant. Should hev ye on the tele.

Ma   Ridges estate! What are wi? Just a joke. Ridges estate! Them that keeps thor coals in the bath. Go to a store for credit. Ridges estate? The' don't want ti know. Go for a decent job. Ridges estate? No chance.

Davy   How come A got that interview then?

Ma   That proves yor somethin' special, Davy. Somebody seen ye were dif'rent. Somebody's took a fancy ti ye.

Davy   Hold on, Ma. Don't want nobody fancyin' us.

Ma   Son, it's yor chance in life. Ye don't want a dead-end job. Toss away all your education. All that study. Don't let yourself down, Davy, an' don't let me down.

Davy   Ma, yor not on. Things isn't like that now.

Ma   Like what?

Davy   Gettin' a good job in an office. Security, all that jazz. That went out wi' trams. Thor's better money on the docks.

Ma   Aye, an' how long will that last? Thor clawin' each other's back now, for a share o' the meat.

Davy   A can get twenty pounds a week startin' money on the quay.

Ma   Little apples, Davy. That's yor da talkin', an' it's little apples.

Davy   An' extras.

Ma   What extras?

Davy   A bit fiddle.

Ma (*outraged*)   Fiddle! What's a laddie like you talkin' about fiddle?

Davy   Nowt wrong wi fiddle. Not like pinchin', it's just . . .
fiddle. Da says every job on the quay has ti have a fiddle, or
the' cannot keep the men.

Ma   Well, it sounds more like Mantovani's bloody
orchestra ti me.

Davy   Aw, Ma!

Ma   Now look, A'm havin' no argument. You were
brought up ti touch nothin' that doesn't belong ye. Yor
keepin' away from it. The fish quay is nowt but the home o'
the forty thieves, an' A nivvor brought ye into the world ti
be a fiddler.

Offstage, **Da** *can be heard returning. He is a robust, friendly man,
only aggressive when frustrated. Heavy with drink, he is singing. His
pocket bulges with a bottle of brown ale and with his filleting knife
wrapped in a cloth. The sleeves of his jacket are sawn off at the elbows,
in the manner of all fish filleters, to keep them from dipping in the
trough.*

Da   'It's not unusual ti be loved by anyone, da dee dee da.'

The door opens and **Da** *enters. He resonantly belches.*

Ma   That's lovely! Lovely A must say. Gi yor family the
benefit o' yor company.

Da (*smiling with the satisfaction of the belch*)   That's me. That's
yor da. Why give it away ti strangers. (*He advances on* **Ma**.
Takes hold of her in a clumsy embrace. Forces her to dance. Sings.)
'Strangers in the night, da, da, dee, da, strangers in the
night.'

Ma (*forces herself free*)   Gerroff, ye great puddin'.

She goes off into the kitchen. **Da** *takes off his jacket, puts it round the
back of his chair and plants his bottle of brown ale on the table.*

Da   Puttin' that kettle on or what?

Ma (*off*)   A'm puttin' the kettle on.

Da   Warra woman. Hellow, Davy! That's my bonny lad. (*Ruffles his son's hair.*) All right, son?

Davy   All right, Da.

Da (*lowering his voice*)   Hey! See them haddocks we were cuttin'. Eh? (*He demonstrates with his hands an approximate eight-inch length.*) A says ti Bob Wilson, what di ye call these? He says, 'Haddocks.' A says, 'Haddocks, ye mean dog's dicks.' A'm no kiddin', the' were no bigger'n dog's dicks.

Ma *comes back in carrying a teapot, just in time to catch the obscenity of the remark.*

Ma   Do you hev ti use language like that an' yor own bit lassie sittin' there?

Da   Ooo! listen sanctimonious! Hey! There's a big word, eh? Sang titty monious. Hey, Ma, yor all right, till you get sang titty monious.

Ma   Gawd! (*She moves back into the kitchen. From this point onwards she goes back and forward from living room to kitchen laying the table.*)

Da   Hellow, Alice. (*He leans over and cuddles her.*) My little lass. (*He goes and looks in the sideboard drawer for a bottle opener.*) My little stay-all-day-in-the-house Alice. All right, pet?

Ma   She stays in all day, 'cos she's given up fightin' sixty other bairns for a share o' the street.

Da   All right, Ma. All right. A'm just sayin' hellow!

Ma   Hev ye seen hor leg? Are ye bothered? Twelve stitches in, from the raggy end of a bottle.

Da   A know. A know! Still! She's got ti learn ti stick up for horsel'. (*To* **Alice**.) You stick up for yorsel', pet. Fightin's natural, an' us is a fightin' family. Wi nivvor give up. Nivvor! You show 'em. (*He sits.*)

Ma   Huh!

Da   A telled ye what General Montgomery sayed to us.

Ma Not that again. (*She disappears into the kitchen.*)

Da (*rising up*) General Mongomery (*calling out to* **Ma**) personally ti me. (*To the kids.*) S'fact! Standin' as near ti me as you are now. Ganna be this big do on, oot in the desert, y'know. Well, all the top brass was round ti gi' the lads a clap on the back. 'Corporal Rutter, 9268754, Royal Northumberland Fusiliers, sor.' Mongomery says, 'Kerprel,' 'Kerprel,' 'e says, 'Course he had this funny way o' talkin', 'cos he's Irish, y'know. 'Kerprel,' 'e says, 'you'se Geordies is fighters.' That's what 'e says, 'Fighters.' That was the famous general, Sir Bernadette Montgomery. Give wi all fifty tabs a piece. Couldn't smoke 'em. Bloody horrible. Owld bastard. But 'Fighters', pet, that what 'e sayed. So you show them, Alice. Anyhow, Ma, where's the rest o' the bairns?

Ma (*returning*) One in the pram ootside, ye probably fell ower hor withoot noticin'.

Da Now, Ma, canny on. No rows, eh? We want no rows.

Ma What di ye want? A roll call? Yor other three's out roamin' the railway. In the hands o' God, or the neighbours, whichever's the worst.

Da Well, the bloody railway! They've never mended that fence. Not since the bairns took it down for Guy Fawkes. But look, pet, A'm home for a bit o' peace an quiet. So let's have no rows, eh? That grub comin' or what?

Ma (*vehemently*) It's comin'.

She leaves. **Da** *pours himself the beer. There is a pause.*

Da That's my Davy. All right, son. Yor a good'n. Hey, no kiddin', ye did yor da proud this mornin'. (**Ma** *comes in to catch the comment.*) Ooo' sorry. (*Absurd gesture of secrecy.*) Nuff sed!

Davy S'all right, Da. She knows A was on the quay.

Ma Yor encouragin' him to go down there.

Da   Me?

Ma   Yes, you.

Da   Not me.

Ma   Fine example you are.

Da   Ma, A've telled ye. That laddie's got his own mind ti make up. He'll do what he wants ti do, and gan where he wants ti gan.

Ma   He's goin' for that interview.

Da   What interview?

Ma   Ye know fine well what interview. The Town Clerk's.

Da (*scornfully*)   Toon Clerk's.

Ma   Yes, the Toon Clerk's an he's goin' for that interview.

Da   Ye've sayed that already.

Ma   And I'm sayin' it again. So he knows where he stands. (*She goes back into the kitchen making a decisive clatter of crockery.*)

Da (*calling after her*)   Ma, wor Davy's a sunshine lad. Y'know. 'E likes it oot in the fresh air, where the seagulls is flying roond. Huh, thor's no bloody seagulls in the Toon Clerk's.

Ma (*off*)   'Course thor's not, ye dope. What would the' be wantin' wi seagulls. Dirty, shitty things.

Da (*taken aback by the vehemence*)   That grub comin', or what.

Ma (*off*)   A've telled ye it's comin'.

Da   So's Chris'mas.

Ma   Alice, come here, giv's a hand.

Alice *goes through to the kitchen to help bring in the plates of food.*

Da (*to* **Davy**)   Tell ye what. She'll have you in a bowler hat, wi' stripy pants.

Davy   Not me.

Da   Gi' yor mates a laugh.

Davy   Not likely.

Da   Toon Clerk's! Call that work? Ye bugs! Sittin' on thor
backsides all day, pushin' a pen. Work! Hey! See what me
an big Mutt lifted on the Grimsby wagon, eh? Ten ton! Ten
bloody ton! Box, by box. None o' yor fancy fork-lifts.
Hundredweight, by hundredweight. Aye, an' the rain
beatin' on wi. Now, that's what ye call work. Not a writer
born, can write that down.

Ma (*off*)   What ye sayin' to him?

Da (*calling back*)   Trouble we' you, Ma, ye place too much
store on education. Yor tryin' ti be upstairs, an' doonstairs
at the same time. An' what di yet get? Stuck on the landin'.

Davy *and* **Da** *enjoy the joke.* **Ma** *comes in with the food and they all
gather at the table.* **Ma** *plants* **Da***'s plateful savagely in front of him.*

Ma   Just fill yor gob wi' chips, and let's have the biggest
relief since Dunkirk. That bairn's goin' ti make use o' his
education.

Da   Education!

Ma   Alice! Davy! Sit down, get yor grub.

Da   A'll tell ye somethin' about education. (*He speaks
between mouthfuls of food.*) It's no good ti the workin' class.
Thor's two kinds of education. The kind the give ti us, and
the kind the keep for thorselves. An' the kind the give ti us,
yor better off withoot.

Ma   What do you know about education?

Da   Don't talk to me about education.

Ma   What would be the point?

Da   Listen, what di ye think the idea is? So's we can better
worselves? Don't kid on. Listen, the idea of education, is ti

make the likes of us useful ti the buggars that's gettin' the
money. Education! Education don't make the job fit you.
Education makes you fit the job. Listen, them desks in the
Toon Clerk's was there long before he was born.

Ma   Jus' gerron wi' yor dinners, take no notice.

Da   Eh? What did ye say? Take no notice . . . Don't you
tell them ti take no notice o' me. (*Everyone stops eating. She has
pushed* **Da** *too far.*) There's a fine . . . What ye mean, tellin'
them that, eh? (*Shouting, half rising and pointing his finger at* **Ma**.)
Don't you bloody tell them ti take no notice o' me. What a
thing ti say. A'm tellin' them summick important. Don't you
tell them ti take no notice o' me.

There's a stunned silence. **Da** *sits and moodily begins to eat. He looks
up at them.*

All right! All right! Gerron wi' yor dinners. Education! Puts
ye at a desk, or on a machine, an' that's what's wrong wi'
this country. Too many machines, an' too many in bloody
offices. (*They resume eating. He speaks to his son.*) Tell ye what,
put me on a machine once. Aye! one o' them fork-lift trucks.
Hey' laugh. Well, A could manage it all right. No bother.
Switch it on. Into gear! Giddup! A went off along the factory
floor . . . an' strite thro' the bloody office. (**Davy** *and* **Da** *and*
Alice *laugh.* **Ma** *doesn't think it's funny.*) Hey', that fettled
them. A says . . . A says, 'A'm sorry, but A don't think A've
quite got the hang of it.' Eeee! ye bugs, laugh! 'Gerris cards.'
'Gerrim out.' But what A'm tryin' to tell ye, son, the laddie
that's drivin' that truck now, what's he pickin' up, eh? A
manky thirty-five pound fifty. Why, it's washers. Look, look.
A'll show ye. (**Da** *rises up and fishes into his hip pocket. He brings
out a roll of money.*) See that. See that handful. Sixty-four quid.
Eh? How's that? Casual! In the hand! Sixty-four quid.
That's what yor da picked up this week. Wi no education,
son, ye might be no good ti nobody but yorsel', but it leaves
ye we' no choice but ti get on. (**Da** *reaches round for his jacket.
He removes his filleting knife from the pocket and unrolls the cloth
covering it.*) Look, A'll show ye. There ye are. That's all ye

need, a good filleting knife. That's the instrument. Carve yousel' a career.

Ma   What di ye want, bringing a wicked thing like that here?

Da   That's how ye cut 'em. (*He demonstrates the filleting of a fish.*)

Ma   Put it away.

Da   A mean it's a simple thing a knife. Eh? But what was ever invented that's more effective?

Ma   Will ye put it away.

Suddenly and alarmingly **Da**'*s temper changes. The kids are frightened. The knife has the appearance of a dagger.*

Da   Will you shut yor silly hole. Shurrup! Shurrup! A'm talkin' ti them. Tryin' ti tell them somethin'. Ye's never listen to us, none o' ye.

Davy   A really fancy the inshore fishin', Da, if A could get –

Da   You as well, shurrup! Never bloody listen. That's another thing about education, gettin' them that's had it to shurrup. (**Davy** *gets up from his chair and walks away from his father.* **Da** *watches him go and lumbers unsteadily after him.*) Now look, Davy! . . . Son! Don't you walk away from me. (**Davy** *slumps into the big easy chair.*) 'Cos A'm tellin' ye . . . (**Davy** *ignores his father.* **Da** *attempts to rationalise.*) Look, A sayed there was two kinds of education. Aye, well there's another sort of education, an' it's the sort ye get for yorsel'. Look! Look! (*It's almost as though he would embrace his son.*) Bob Wilson! Take Bob Wilson! Y'know Bob. Eh? Comes cryin' ti me. Right? Got fifty boxes on his hands, right? Y'know, cod, haddock, plaice, what have ye. Right? How much, Bob? How much? Fifty pence a box? Not on. Not on, Bob. Sixty pence a box. Seventy pence a box. Ye want them filleted? Eighty pence a box. He's over a barrel, see? A squeeze the sod. A've got this. (*He brandishes the knife.*) Aye, an' A can use it. A'm a skilled man. the' need me. Hev knife, will travel, an' thor's no arguin' wi' the uneducated. (*He goes back to the table and picks up the rolls of notes.*) Look, son, look. Sixty-four quid. Not bad, eh? If you can do like yor da, son, we'll be rollin'. (*He throws the roll of notes over to* **Ma**. *She pushes them away from her.*)

Ma   Aye, an' where's yor sixty-four quids on the lay-off weeks? When thor's no fish comin' in. What about the weeks wi' nowt?

Da   Woman! It's the rough wi' the smooth.

Ma   Yor brains is locked behind iron bars. It's not a matter o' money.

Da *furiously sweeps the money and half the table crockery on to the floor.*

Da   Ivvorythin's a matter o' money. Ivvorythin's a matter o' money. (*He leaps to his feet.*)

Davy   Don't, Da. Don't.

Ma   Ye great destructive beast. It's a matter o' livin' like people, not animals. Alice, go away ootside, an' mind that bairn.

Alice *scatters out of the room.*

Da   What's the matter, is the money not good enough for ye?

Ma   No, it's not.

Da   What more di ye want?

Davy   Don't, man, Da. Don't.

Da   Shurrup. What more di ye want?

Ma   A'll tell ye what A want. A want the bairns brought up decent, an' not hearin' their mother shoutin' blue murder ti the neighbours every Saturday night.

Da   Gerraway ti hell. Stuffin' their heads wi' that rubbish. An' what difference would it make to us where wi lived? An' di ye think the wives in posh houses don't shout blue murder. Aye, maybes the' do it quieter, 'cos they've been educated ti be polite. An' if the neighbours heard them, they'd be ower polite to listen.

During **Da***'s speech* **Ma** *has begun to pick up the scattered debris from the floor.*

Davy   Da!

Da   Leastways ye've always got that fanny Ann from over the path ti come round slaverin' sympathy. (*Mocking.*) 'What's the matter, pet, has he been beltin' ye?' 'Is 'e away doon ti Charlie's again?' 'Eee poor soul, what ye have ti put up with.'

Davy   Da, lay off.

Da   It makes ye bloody sick. (*Thumps the table.*) Us is born, an' bred in this Ridges estate, an' thor's no changin' that. An' thor's no changin' us. (*To* **Davy**.) An' the sooner she gets the daft ideas out of hor head the better. (*Closes up on* **Ma**.) Look! Ye want that laddie ti better hisself, eh? that what ye want? Well, let him go where the money is.

Ma   You, ye pull everythin' down ti your level.

Da   An' you. You! Ye'd turn me own bairns against us.

Davy   Da, man, leave it be.

Da   Turn me own bairns against us. 'Cos ye haven't the sense ti be content with what ye have.

Ma   Be content with what A have!

Da   Yes.

Ma   What is it A've got? Go on, tell us.

Da   Ye've got a bloody roof over yor heed for a start.

Ma   A've ti be greatful for that? Is it all right livin' an behavin' like pigs, as long as w'are dry pigs?

Da   Yor mother an' father were glad of a roof over thor head.

Ma   Aye, me mother an' father come out o' the low street. Yes, they were slum clearance, but the' were happy.

Da (*with contempt*)   Happy!

Ma   Yes, happy! That's somethin' thor's no room for here. Like thor's no room for hope, an' no room for love.

Da   Love! (*As though it were a sick word.*) Ye great soft bitch. What's that got ti do with it?

Davy   Don't, Da.

Ma   Aye, A'm a soft bitch. Found that out the night A married you, an' yor mates carried ye upstairs.

Da   A've given ye six bairns.

Ma   Yes, mevves yor not fit ti drive a fork-lift truck but thor's one job ye proved yorsel' on.

Da   That's right, get yor bloody joke in.

Ma   It's no joke. But yor not top o' the league. Upstairs has given his soft bitch nine, next door has got eight, and the soft bitch ower the path has ten up ti now.

Da   What's that got ti do wi' me, ye daft bat?

Ma   It's what A'm sayin', yor not responsible. Ye've no more talent that what it takes ti fillet a fish, but yor allowed ti run yor own private orphanage, an' ye've got it that crowded thor queuein' for the netty.

Infuriated and still wielding the knife, **Da** *lunges at* **Ma**.

Da   Ye talk a load o' rubbish.

Davy *darts across, grabs his father by the arm and hangs on fiercely.*

Davy   Da! Da!

Da   Nowt but a load o' rotten rubbish. All the time, rubbish! Rubbish! (*He tries to break free of* **Davy**.)

Davy   Da! A've gotta job! A've gotta job, Da.

Da *looks at* **Davy** *uncomprehendingly.*

Da   What you talkin' about? Job! Job! What job? (*He calms down.*)

Davy   A've gotta job, Da. Bob Wilson set us on.

Da   Eh?

Davy   Gotta job on the quay wi' Bob Wilson.

Ma   Davy, what ye sayin'?

Davy   A'm sorry, Ma.

Ma   Davy!

Da   What ye talkin' about, Bob sayed nothin' ti me.

Davy   Right enough, Da. After ye'd gone 'e asked us if A wanted a start.

Ma   Ye see. Ye see what ye've done.

Da   A've told ye, woman, A know nothin' about it. (*To* **Davy**.) Look, A'm yor father. Now A'm entitled to know what's goin' on.

Davy   He's startin' four school leavers on Monday. He's got three. He asked us if a wanted the job. Twenty pounds a week.

Da   Oh Davy, what ye done?

Davy   Twenty pounds, Ma. It's ownly twelve at the Town Clerk. It's another eight quid.

Pause.

Da   Well, A know nothin' about it. Nothin'. (*Pause.*) Anyhow, what's Bob wantin' wi' four young laddies?

Davy   He's puttin' a machine in.

Da   Machine? What machine?

Davy   A filletin' machine, Da.

There is a pause as **Da** *struggles with the news.*

Da   A what?

Davy   A filletin' machine, Da. Bob says ye just feed the fish in, it goes thro' the machine, an' comes out the other end all cut.

Da   A know what a filletin' machine is.

Davy   There's no experience necessary.

Pause.

Da   Ye bugs. Nobody tells ye nothin' ti yor face.

Davy   Bob says thor installin' it this weekend. 'E reckons it'll cut fifty stone an hour.

Pause.

Da   Why is it? Nobody tells ye nothin' ti yor face.

Davy   Reckons it's fantastic. Even small fish. Just rattles them thro'.

Da   S'what gets me. The' cannot come out with it.

Davy   Has these nylon gears.

Da   Fifty stone an hour, eh?

Davy   That's what Bob says.

Da   Aye, well, that's more'n a filleter's day's work.

Davy   Bob says the blades are –

Da   Oh, ti hell wi' what Bob says.

Pause.

Ma   Davy! Get away out.

Davy   What's the matter, Ma?

Ma   Go on, get away out.

Davy   What've A done? A mean –

Ma   Just get away out, Davy. Don't bother your da.

Davy (*disgruntled*)   A dunno! What we' always fightin' for?

He leaves and **Da** *slumps in a chair.*

Da   Nivvor ti yor face, that's what gets me. If they'd just come an' tell ye ti yor face.

Ma *resumes her tidying up.*

Ma   Some things the' cannot say to a man's face.

Da   There was talk, like – ye know. Thor's always talk. But nobody ever comes out straight with it.

Ma   A'll pour ye out a fresh cup o' tea.

Da   No. Don't bother.

Ma   It's no bother. Look, it's still hot.

Da   No it's all right. Look . . . (*Awkward pause.*) I'm sorry about the mess.

Ma   It's all right. Big seas rock the little boats.

She pours him out a fresh cup of tea. He is hunched over and she has to go close to him to offer the tea. This is a moment of truth. Despite the abusive row, when the chips are down, **Ma** *is the support figure.*

Here!

Da   Ta!

He takes the tea with one hand. With his other hand he reaches her . . . He does not drink his tea but nurses it in his hands. The door opens and **Alice** *enters.*

Ma   Told you ti stay out an' mind the bairn.

Alice   Met Danny Mac. Sent us up with a message for Da.

Da   Message? What message?

Alice   'E says, 'Tell yor da from Bob Wilson, not ti bother comin' down on Monday, 'cos thor's nowt expected.'

Pause. **Da** *looks pathetically at* **Ma**. *He is shattered.*

Da   Ye buggar! Eh! Danny Mac! What's the matter wi' them? Bob tells Danny Mac. Danny Mac he tells her. What's the matter, the' cannot come and tell me ti me face?

Ma   Mevves be a bit hard ti tell a man to his face . . . (*regretting what she is committed to say*) that he's not wanted.

Da *rouses himself to salvage his pride. He gets up from his chair and grabs his jacket.*

Da   What's 'e say? Nowt expected. Is that what 'e says? Aye, well, that's what they bloody think.

He storms out. **Ma** *resumes clearing up.*

Ma   Was the bairn asleep?

Alice   Yes.

Ma   Better off, stayin' with her dreams. Look, help us clear up this mess. All them papers strewed there, pick them up. There's a good lass. Stuff them back on the mantelpiece, the' might be important.

Alice *complies but then stops to study her school report which she discovers on the mantelpiece.*

Ma   What ye readin'?

Alice   Nothin'.

Ma   Nothin'?

Alice   Jus' me school report.

Ma   Let's have a look.

Alice   What for?

Ma   Let's have a look. A want ti see it. (**Alice** *hands it over.*) 'Maths – lacks con-cen-tration. English – some

improvement this term. Hist'ry – capable of better. Music –'
didn't knaa ye took music.

Alice   Oh aye.

Ma   'Music – shows considerable, apt- apti-' – What's this
word?

Alice   Aptitude.

Ma   Well, that's good, isn't it?

Alice   S'pose so.

Ma   An' you've got it considerable. Well, that's nice, Alice.
You know, it's a good thing ti be good at is music. Mevves
ye should take it up. Learn the piana.

Alice   Yor jokin', Ma.

Ma   No, A'm not jokin', luv. Music's a luvely thing ti hev.
Somethin' A always fancied meself, learnin' the piana.

Alice   Where'd we get a piana?

Ma   Thor ownly fifty pence a week. A was thinkin' about
doin' a bit part-time again. They'd have us back in the shop
any time. Yes, music, that's a good thing ti have, Alice.

Alice   What would the' say round here if the' heard we
had a piana?

Ma   The' wouldn't mind that. Folks like a bit o' music.
Why, yor welcome anywhere if ye can play an instrument. It
brings pleasure. Well, it's not just for yorself, this apt-, apti- –

Alice   Aptitude.

Ma   Aye. Well, that means it's like a gift. Summick ye've
got inside ye. Summick that's all yor own. But ye can share
it. Ye understand, pet. But when ye hev summick inside ye,
ye hev ti do somethin' about it. 'Cos it's always like waitin',
wantin' ti be brought out into the light.

Alice *does not believe anything. She switches on her radio and there is music. She picks up her comic and immerses herself in it.* **Ma** *looks helplessly at her.*

You Are My Heart's Delight

C. P. Taylor

You Are My Heart's Delight was first performed by Live Theatre Company in 1977, with the following cast:

David   Colin MacLachlan
Janet   Annie Orwin

Directed by Paul Chamberlain
Designed by Phil Bailey

Editor's Note

There are many C. P. Taylor plays produced by Live Theatre Company which might have been included in this anthology. This short piece didn't gain the prominence of some of his other work such as *Bandits*, *A Nightingale Sang in Eldon Square*, *Bring Me Sunshine* or *Operation Elvis*, but it captures much of Cecil's humility and gentle anarchy.

Director Paul Chamberlain had put together an interesting tour of both rural and smaller town venues throughout the Northern region – a departure for the company, whose work had until then been mainly urban in identity. The programme, designed specifically for the tour in terms of theme and subject matter, consisted of three half-hour pieces, including *You Are My Heart's Delight*, as well as *The Pigeon Man* by Tom Hadaway and *Phantom of the Fells* by Michael Wilcox. Tim Healy was in both Tom and Michael's pieces and this beautiful, funny, sad play provides fond memories of spending the late summer of 1977 touring the beautiful countryside of Northumberland, Durham and Cumbria.

A cottage in the borders of Scotland. Recently modernised by the estate management. Telly in the corner. Modern fireplace, contrasting with the heavy, old-fashioned furniture. A fish tank.

Janet *is dividing her time between preparing the tea and cutting out figures from a mail-order catalogue. She sticks the pages to odd pieces of cardboard and after they have dried, cuts out the figures. Completed figures are displayed all round the room, on the mantelpiece, on the sideboard as ornaments.*

It's late spring. Evening. **Janet** *hears* **David** *approaching and concentrates on her cooking.* **David** *enters. He carries a shotgun, which he puts down carefully. He takes off his coat and boots, then begins to clean his gun, watching* **Janet**. *He is clearly disturbed about something.*

David   Good smell. (*He looks at the catalogue on the table.*)

Janet   Mince roll.

David   Andrew told me he'd brought you a new catalogue.

Janet   Some bonnie things in it, David. (*Showing him.*) I just cut that out . . .

David   There's something left in the bottle, isn't there?

Janet   You know better than me what's left in the bottle.

David (*going over to the sideboard and pouring himself a glass of whisky – his hand is shaking*)   You couldn't say I had any temper to us, could ye? That's one thing nobody could say against me.

Janet   All you need to do, David. I told you . . . is get Sir Malcolm on one of his clear days. And tell him how much that gate's bothering you. He'd put –

David   It's nothing to do with the gate, woman! Who says it's anything to do with the gate!

Janet   Look at you, just now. Going at the spirits.

David I said to Mr Charles. Last year. We're losing partridges by the hundred along the Berwick Road. Getting mowed down, right, left and centre. If we rented the shooting rights to a syndicate, we'd have enough money for proper fencing along the whole of the estate running by the Berwick Road.

Janet Did Andrew tell you he had to stop Sir Malcolm driving through the village, this morning?

David Sir Malcolm's saner than you or me. His mind's sharper than ever. He's over much on his mind, that's the problem. Mr Charles has him running round in circles . . . the way he's mucking about with the estate . . .

Janet Sir Malcolm was driving on the wrong side of the road. Half on the pavement . . .

David He's a lawyer, Mr Charles. What the hell does a bloody lawyer know about running an estate like this!

Janet Andrew said Sir Malcolm probably thought he was driving in France or somewhere . . . Where they drive on the wrong side of the road.

David I never wanted a tar road up to the cottage. It happened, exactly as I told Sir Malcolm it would . . .

Janet Will I give you your soup now, David?

David I haven't finished my gun, have I? Ye want me te put it away with all the filth of the day's work.

. . . I told him: you put a tar road up to the cottage, and you'll have every Tom, Dick and Harry coming up to the moors . . .

Janet (*watching the gun being cleaned*) If you told Sir Malcolm how that gate's getting on your nerves, David . . . It wouldn't cost all that much to put a cattle grid in its place.

David Tearing up the land on either side of the road. All that disturbing the earth. We haven't had a snipe on the

moor, now, within a mile of where they've been working . . .
Took near a year to get the badger back again.

Janet   I mean. There's no need for it, David. Coming
back every night, all worked up like that. Over the gate.
When all you need to do is to tell Sir Malcolm –

David   I'm not worked up about the gate, woman! I told
you! It's nothing to do with the bloody gate! (*Finishing cleaning
his gun.*)

Janet (*eyes on the gun*)   Did you thin the coots on
Sweethope?

David (*putting the gun away*)   I'll take my soup now, Janet.

Janet   Aye . . . Have it now, David. I'm starving. Waiting
for you . . .

David (*holding the gun for a moment, before he replaces it in the gun
cabinet*)   I took seventy coots from Sweethope . . . Single-
handed . . . Mr Charles wouldn't dirty his hands on a job
like that. Doubt if he can shoot anyway. There's still forty-
odd left. Wasted half the morning spelling it all out to him,
why the loch needed thinning out. Left to him, he wouldn't
have taken one!

Janet   I can understand him. I like the sight of the loch full
of coots. They've *life* in them . . . Haven't they, David?
(*Putting down his soup.*)

David   It was *Mr Charles* that gave me the van. Sir
Malcolm would have never given me a van. I never wanted
a van.

Janet   You know what we had at the table this morning,
David? A nuthatch . . .

David   I can'ne *talk* to *Him*! You can'ne get through to
him. He keeps shouting about natural control . . . Coots'll
control themselves in the end. The Partridges that've
learned the trick of crossing the Berwick Road without
getting flattened by heavy lorries'll go onte raise chicks with

that knack, too. He's driving everybody like mad. Planting the woods. Draining fields. Building new roads. Paying me to keep his estate. And he keeps on shouting about *natural control*!

Janet (*apropos of the soup*)   Ye like it?

David   It's fine . . . See . . . He can'ne grasp it. This is not a *natural* estate. Is it? Any estate. It's not natural.

Janet   He came right on the table . . . The nuthatch . . . Bonnie, David . . .

David   He's due about, now . . .

Janet   Was he no' a wee bit later last year? Have ye had words with Mr Charles, then?

David   Benny Hill's on the night, is he?

Janet   Tomorrow night . . . *Softly Softly*'s on . . . That you like.

David   One of these days . . . These catalogue people. They'll get on to ye. Won't they? Ye keep getting them to send ye catalogues . . . and ye never buy anything out of them.

Janet   I like them. I like looking though them, David.

David   They could get ye for that. Couldn't they? They talk about the catalogues being worth four or five pounds . . . don't they? . . . They could ask the money for them.

Janet (*protectively at her catalogue*)   It says . . . when you write away for them. Under no obligation.

David   I was going to shoot at this lorry . . . for God's sake, Janet . . . on the Berwick Road . . . God knows what the hell stopped us. Had the safety catch off.

Janet   At a man? Ye were never going to shoot at a man, for God's sake, David?

David   I never said I was shooting at a man. At a lorry. I said. I was aiming at his tyres. Couldn'e tell ye te this minute what the hell stopped my finger on the trigger . . .

Janet   He must've riled ye, David. To shoot at him.

David   God, maybe. Something . . . beyond us . . .

She waits for him to continue. He indicates his empty soup plate.

I'm ready for my mince, Janet.

Janet   I'm getting it for you . . .

David   You could buy something from them . . . couldn't you? For once . . . From the catalogue. To stop them from taking it up. You getting catalogues and never buying anything.

Janet   What did you take your gun to him for, David?

David   To the lorry driver . . . Streak of evil . . . answering, evil . . . That's what it was . . . Some of the things that happen on the Berwick Road. They're accidents plain and simple . . . But some of them . . . it's a streak of evil.

I'm walking along the big field . . . skirting the Berwick Road. A few minutes back. I just found a sandpiper with a full clutch . . . by the river . . . Just going through the gate. Back to the road and my van. And there's this hen partridge. Twelve chicks on her tail. Crossing the Berwick Road.

Janet   David . . . I can'ne stand hearing about things like that . . . !

David   You asked me to tell you what took my gun to my shoulder . . . didn't you . . . Ye know how partridges take their time crossing . . . Dawdlin' across. One chick stuck on the bank. The mother callin' her. Half a mile off. This big lorry. Quarter a mile. Dry road. Clear sight of her. That bit . . . The road's straight near a mile . . . isn't it . . . Belting . . .

Sixty an hour. Seventy . . . maybe . . . this wee raft of chicks
. . . and the mother . . .

Janet   David!

David   He couldn't miss seeing them. A line of them. If
his eyes were on the road, he couldn't miss seeing them. See
from his face, woman, he'd the sight of them. And I was
there. With my arm up, shouting to him to stop. Hen started
panicking . . . then, now . . . could see . . . Putting his foot
down harder . . . more like it . . . then taking it off . . .
Bloody ploughed right through the raft of chicks – Right
through them . . .

Janet   It's just killing . . . People killing . . .

David   That wee raft of life. On the road . . . Him just
throwing himself at it. Never even stopping for me. Had my
gun up . . . and my sight on his back tyre . . .

Janet   You could've killed him. If he had a burst at that
speed, couldn't you . . .

David   Was'ne thinking of anything . . . But putting a
cartridge inte that bloody monster . . . Stinking exhaust . . .
spittin' filth and noise . . . just filling the air with filth and
noise . . . wherever it went . . . and killing . . .

Janet   You could've, couldn't you . . .

David   God knows how . . . The mother came out of it . . .
and four chicks.

Janet   Thank God, David, you never fired . . .

David   See . . . The minute before he turned up . . . It was
such a bonny afternoon . . . wasn't it?

Janet   Like summer . . .

David   And I'd been watching the sandpiper on her eggs
. . . And then seeing the partridges . . . Watching them with
their mother . . . All that life jumping in them . . . In wee
things like that . . . There's so much life jumping inside of

them . . . Isn't there? . . . And that bastard comes along with his bloody monster! . . .

Janet   At least there's four of them left, David. And the mother . . .

David   A wee bit salty. (*Indicating mince.*)

Janet   Is it? . . . Should'ne be . . .

David   It's all right . . .

Janet   Do you want to see what I got in the order from Patterson's . . . Wee treat for you . . . (*Going to sideboard.*) Wee box of chocolates . . . the dark ones . . . you like . . .

David   You like the milk ones . . .

Janet   I don't mind either . . . Thought we'd have a treat . . . While we're watching *Softly Softly* . . . eh, David?

David   It's no' my birthday . . . Is it?

Janet   You know fine it isn't . . .

David   I lose track of it . . . It's soon . . .

Janet   Soon . . .

David   I'm over it, now, Janet . . .

Janet   I know.

David   It was being so near to shooting at him . . .

Janet   De ye think I *should* maybe get something from the catalogue, David? For once?

David   If there's something takes your fancy. Why shouldn't you?

Janet   What do you think I should get?

David   You know what you need yourself, don't you?

Janet   No . . . But the way you were talking before . . .

David   Just a change . . . From these dresses and that you get at Coldstream . . . That's all I was thinking about . . . Some of them . . . Ye cut out . . .

Janet   Like one of these. (*Indicating the cut-out models around the room.*)

David   Just whatever ye fancy . . .

Janet   They're just for young lassies, David!

David   Not all of them . . .

Janet   If folks saw us in one of them . . .

David   Who'd see you here . . . Eight miles up the hill . . . Anyway?

Janet   Would you like to see us in one of these, David?

David   It's up to you . . . I don't know anything about dresses . . . Be a change, wouldn't it?

Janet   I'll make you a cup of tea, now . . . Will I?

David (*looking at the chocolates*)   Isn't there chocolates ye can buy . . . milk and plain . . . ? (*As he is talking the lights go off.*) I think I saw them on the television . . . What have ye done there, Janet? Put the light on, woman!

Janet   Have'ne touched it, David . . . It's just gone out . . .

David   He ye fused it. Putting in the kettle.

Janet   Just filling the kettle. I'm no' near the plug.

David   Be a fuse somewhere.

Janet (*with a torch*)   I'll get the fuse wire.

David   I'm sure there's these chocolates. Dark and white.

Janet   Have you been at the fuse wire, David? It was in the top drawer here.

David   Wait a minute. I was using it for the van. For a bad connection. I brought it back in again.

Janet   I've got a screwdriver . . .

David   God! Where the hell did I put it?

Janet   I'll light one of the lamps, just now . . . (*She gets out an oil lamp, and lights it.*)

David   I'll just use some of this flex . . . See . . . Strip it down . . . and use that, the now . . . Do. Till the morning.

Janet   Sure. It'll be safe.

David   Got the wire cutters . . . ?

Janet   They're all in the top drawer . . .

David *strips the wire, separates the strands.*

Janet   I'll get the steps.

Janet *brings out stepladders, puts them against the wall to let* **David** *reach the fuse box.*

David   That'll do.

Janet   I'll hold the ladder . . .

David *mounts the ladder, screwdriver in hand, wire.*

David   Can ye hold the torch right up . . . Higher . . . That's fine. (*Takes out a fuse and examines it . . .*) NOT that one . . . (*Replaces it, about to take another one when he draws back his hand.*) Janet . . .

Janet   Have'ne given yersel' a shock, have ye?

David   I'm just thinkin' . . . Will we leave it, the night? . . . Just for the night (*He looks at her.*) We've got the lamps . . . We've had the electric light night after night. Nine months running . . .

Janet   Just . . . Not fix it, David? . . .

David   Night after night.

Janet   What about the kettle . . . David? Ye have'ne had yer tea, yet?

David   We've got the old kettle . . . Haven't we? . . . Look at the room . . . in the light of the lamp . . .

Janet   It's bonny . . . Soft . . .

David   We can do without it for one night . . . (*Climbing down.*)

Janet   Ye'll miss *Softly Softly*, David . . .

David (*taking away the stepladder*)   To hell with *Softly Softly*!

Janet *brings out the kettle, goes about organising the tea.* **David** *stands by the gun case.*

David   There's two pair of jays, now. In the Bygate woods.

Janet (*looking at the guns in the case*)   They look nice . . . In that light.

David   Can'ne take two pair of jays. That wood. Bad enough with one . . .

Janet   They're so bonnie.

David   You have'ne seen them tearing away at a nest to get at the eggs or the chicks.

Janet   I saw them at that wren's. Two summers ago. Didn't I?

David   I like the smell. Of the oil.

Janet   I don't mind it.

David   Good smell. There's no other way ye can do it. Keep an estate . . . Is there? . . . Thinnin out the coots, this afternoon . . . It had to be done. Loch would've been covered with them. In a couple of years' time . . . No room for anything else.

Janet   There's your tea. Do you want a chocolate, now, David?

David   I might have. One or two.

Janet Last year or two . . . Sometimes . . . When you turn your head . . .

David Ye get led astray by the bonny feathers. You know what the jay is in a wood . . . A jay's death.

Janet You look like father . . . Just a wee bit.

David How . . . Like . . . In the last year or two . . . What happened in the last year or two to turn me looking like him?

Janet I just said . . . Just . . . a hint . . . A wee bit . . . like . . . It's maybe . . . getting that wee bit older, David.

David (*disturbed at this*) You said that yourself . . . Something you keep saying . . . Age doesn't mean a thing . . . It doesn't . . . The kind of life we have here. Probably does it. I never feel old. Never at any time in my life have I ever thought of you as anything but a young woman . . .

Janet We're not old, David. I'm no' saying we're old . . . We're no' young, either.

David The way you move about the house. And outside. You can run up Murton Law like a young lassie . . . for God's sake . . . Can't you.

Janet I didn't say we were old. Do you like your chocolates?

David They're fine. Got a better taste to them. Take one.

Janet Bought them for you.

David Janet, woman.

Janet I'll take one. Is there a nut one?

David Taste it. (*Getting up.*)

Janet Aye. They're nice.

David Wish we'd had our tea in the oil light. (*From bedroom.*) Have you shifted the gramophone, Janet? I put it under the bed.

Janet   That would be nice. I put it on top of the wardrobe. The records are in a box inside. I'll light you another lamp.

She goes to light another lamp, and takes it to him.

David   I don't feel old . . . Janet . . . Do you? (*From bedroom.*)

Janet   You managing it . . .

David   I'm fine.

He brings in an old acoustic gramophone, sets it on the table.

Janet   I didn'e mean . . . You were anything like father . . . In *nature*, David. You Know That.

David   I'll get the records.

Janet   We're both like mother . . . aren't we . . . Thank God . . . We both get our nature from mother.

David   How long are you going to bear a grudge against a man dead near twenty years, for God's sake.

Janet   That's not bearing a grudge. What I'm saying . . .

David   Twenty years dead . . . and you only had nine years of him . . . anyway . . . hadn't you . . . I had over twenty . . . You got away soon enough to grannie's . . .

Janet   David . . . Honest . . . Whatever he did to us . . . It's forgiven and forgotten long ago.

David   Look at the dust covering it. (*Opening the gramophone lid.*)

Janet   I'll get a duster.

David   God! The things he did to me. When I was a *man* . . . never mind when I was a *boy*, for God's sake . . . The last time I sat at his table . . . He threw a plate of scalding broth at us.

Janet   Forgot we had so many records.

David   What it was, was he was jealous. At us . . . Getting out of Blantyre. Not getting sucked into the pits like him. Ye couldn't blame him, could you? Him stuck in Blantyre. Down the pit six days a week. Me going off to Northumberland. Living in the hills. Out in the sun all day.

Janet   I'm telling you. I've forgotten and forgiven him years back.

David   What do you want on?

Janet   I'll have a look. (*Turning over the records.*)

David   There's nothing to forgive. Even when he was leathering inte me when I was a boy . . . I knew that . . .

Janet   I just said . . . at odd minutes . . . in the light.

David   He was like chained up, woman. To the pit. The pit had him.

Janet *has put on a record of Kathleen Ferrier singing 'Blow the Wind Sotherly'. She stands, listening to it, lost in the song's images.*

David   He was like me. You can't tie me up. There's some folks that can be tied up. I'm not saying it's natural to anybody . . . but some can stand it. Like some animals or birds that can be tamed . . . isn't it? (**Janet** *is listening to the record.*) He was bursting out the pit . . . pulling away . . . That's what made him like he was . . . that's all . . . Tearing himself away . . . and the pit never letting go its hold of him.

Janet   She had cancer when she made that record.

David   That's all his hammerings amounted to . . . isn't it?

Janet   She died not all that long after . . . of cancer . . . Kathleen Ferrier . . .

David   Oh . . . (*Sits listening to the record.*) Never been keen on that. Depresses you . . . to listen to it . . .

Janet   Not me . . . Nothing like that. Other way round.

David (*when record is finished*)   Put something on more like it. (*Puts on Tauber's 'You Are My Heart's Delight'.*)

Janet   Oh . . . that's lovely . . .

David *has gone to the sideboard and is pouring two drinks out from the whisky.*

Janet   Still got my tea, David.

David   Need something better than tea for that.

Janet   We have'ne had that out (*indicating gramophone*) . . . since we got the electricity . . . Have we?

David   Television set . . .

Janet   I never asked for one, David.

David   Couldn't refuse it . . . could you? Sir Malcolm coming all this way to bring it to us.

Janet   I'm not bothered with it . . . If it broke down tomorrow . . . I would'ne lift a finger to do anything about it.

David (*listening to Tauber*)   Get nothing like that on the television.

Janet *listens and drinks.*

David   You see . . . You're cramped up in the van . . . In the morning . . . Driving away down the road . . . And then you come up to the gate . . . Driving along without stopping for miles . . . and then you have this gate . . .

Janet   It's just the one gate, David. I know . . . It gets on your nerves . . . But at the same time . . .

David   You have to stop the car . . . brake . . . get out . . . Open the gate . . . Start up again . . . Stop when you're through . . .

Janet   But before you had the van. You had to walk near eight miles. What I mean . . . is – are you no' letting your imagination get the better of you . . . ?

For a minute **David** *sits back, listens to Tauber, thinking.*

David   To hell with that bloody van.

Janet   You've father's bad language . . . That's one thing you have from him . . .

David   Just leave it in the garage . . . Or give it back to Sir Malcolm . . . I don't want it . . . What the hell do I want a van for . . . Been here twenty years without one . . .

Janet   It was Mr Charles that gave you it . . .

David   What the hell use is it to me . . . ? What use is a gamekeeper, that keeps to the roads all his time, for God's sake.

Janet   Would you give him it back . . . ?

David   I'm telling you. The time I go into Coldstream. It takes any pleasure you have out of going there.

Janet   I enjoy the bus. Seeing folk in the bus.

David   If he wants, Mr Charles can give us a pony . . . But I wouldn'e use that, all that much. Aside from the gate . . . You can see nothing from a van. The noise of it – frightens anything miles ahead of it.

Janet   David. You know something . . . I really feel happy . . . just at the idea of it. Getting rid of it . . . like something was taken off our backs . . .

David   I'm telling you . . . I'll take it back to the estate office, in the morning.

Record finishes.

Have that again, eh?

Janet   It's lovely . . . Could never have enough of that.

David   Lifts you right up, doesn't it. (*Winding up gramophone and putting on Tauber, again.*)

Janet   Do you know what I think it was, David . . . I think it was the electric light. Making you look like father . . .

David   Shut up in the van . . . You don't get any feel of the summer. All ye get is the smell of petrol . . . and the noise of the engine.

Janet   If you explain to Mr Charles you can do your work better without it, David . . .

David   Or the winter . . . or any of the times of the year . . . do you?

Janet   They're nice chocolates.

David   Listen, Janet. This . . . Just now . . .

Janet   I like it. I've always liked the light from oil . . . That electric . . . It hammers on your head . . . Doesn't it?

David   We don't need to fix that fuse, Janet. (*She looks at him, this is something she would never have thought of.*) We can leave it. As it is . . .

Janet   For the night, David, like?

David   Never fix it . . . leave it as it is . . . We've plenty of lamps . . . Easy get oil delivered again . . .

Janet   *Never* fix it.

David   We don't need it . . . We don't need the van . . . and we don't need electricity . . .

Janet   What about the television?

David   Do you need the television?

Janet   It doesn't bother me one way or the other . . . If it's on, I'll watch it . . . if it isn't . . . I've plenty other things to do . . .

David   We're doing fine without it, just now, aren't we?

Janet   It's lovely . . .

David   Can'ne hear yersel' speak at times for it, can ye?

Janet   Would you do that, David . . . Just leave it off . . . ?

David   He had a good week . . . A few months before he died . . . Father . . .

Janet   I know . . .

David   He could've stayed here with us for ever. Had the time of his life. That was his place. Out here . . . with green all around him.

Janet   He was entirely different here . . . wasn't he?

David   I'm telling you . . . He never raised his voice once . . . did he . . . the week he was here.

Janet   I'm happy enough . . . David . . . To do without electricity.

David   Sir Malcolm and Mr Charles meant well, with all these things . . . improvements.

Janet   I forgot all about that week . . . father was here, David. Is that not funny. Till you spoke about it, just now.

David   When you think about it. I'm saying . . . I know he meant it for the good of us . . . But the last year . . . Since we've had all these improvements. I'm thinking about it. Can you remember one thing about it . . . That stands out in your mind?

Janet   Can'ne remember much about the summer. No . . .

David   That's what I mean. Nor the spring. I can remember dozens of things the summer before.

Janet   We had a picnic in Cocksburnpath . . . and you were swimming. That was the year before, wasn't it? That was the year . . . there were wild strawberries . . . covering the place.

David   That night we went down the road . . . and found these two badger bears wiring into each other.

Janet   I remember it was a bad summer . . . That's all I can get.

David   It was a *bad* year . . .

Janet   And the year before . . . two years back . . . I mind things from that . . .

David   It was miserable, wasn't it? That's the only word for it. There was no joy in it. I can'ne call to mind one scrap of joy in the whole year!

Janet   Do you think so, David? (*Thinking.*) It wasn't all that bad, David.

David   Think yourself . . . Neither bad . . . Nor good. There was nothing.

Janet   *Maybe.* The electricity . . . and the van and that. And the gate getting on your nerves.

David   And the room Mr Charles built on.

Janet   My room.

David   We didn't need another room. We were fine as we were, weren't we? We'd been in that room together since we first came here, for God's sake!

Janet, *shaken by the depth of feeling in* **David**'s *voice, sensing where all this is leading.*

Janet   Mr Charles was just doing it for us. To make us more comfortable.

David   We were fine. Weren't we? Tell you the whole thing. All these changes they've thrown at us. You know what they're doing. They're going to make us old before our time. That's what they're going to end up doing! Everything they've given us . . . has turned the whole year sour . . . But the worst was shutting us out from each other with these walls they built . . .

Janet   Do you think they did . . . ?

David I've been on my own all last year, Janet . . . So have you . . . I cann'e stand lying all night on my own . . . I'm cold . . . body and spirit . . . I'm shivering all the night.

Janet David. So am I . . . I'm the same.

David Are you?

Janet I'm telling you.

David That soured the whole year. I'm out all the day, away from you . . . And then being cut off from you at nights.

Janet See – when you go into one room . . . at night . . . and I into the other – it cuts into me.

David Goes right into my stomach.

Janet We'll use that room . . . for storing things . . . eh . . . will we?

David You need somebody beside you at night. It's natural, isn't it?

Janet Listen, David. Will we go to bed . . . now . . . and talk . . . like we used to do?

David Are you tired . . . Janet?

Janet Just to talk. It's nicer and easier talking in bed. I'll make you some cocoa, later . . . like we used to do, and we'll have it in bed.

David They're mad . . . aren't they . . . Some of the things folk do to themselves.

Janet I'll get my night things.

David Will we get ready for bed, here?

Janet That's what we always used to do.

David *goes and fetches his pyjamas.* **Janet** *returns with her nightie. She puts on a record – Schubert's 'An Die Musik'.*

David *comes in, a bit shy. They turn their backs on each other, undress and put on their night things.*

Janet (*when she's ready*)   I'm ready, now . . .

David   Nearly . . .

As he is unbuttoning his jacket, the light suddenly comes on. **Janet** *still doesn't look at* **David**. *He hasn't given the signal. Instead . . . she quickly pulls a chair to the main switch, climbs on it and switches the current off.*

I'm ready . . . (*They turn to each other.*) You see . . . when you're walking . . . The time you get to that gate . . . You've been right through that cut in the Bygate woods . . . And you come up to the gate . . . You're full of the thirty minutes you've been walking . . . The gate's like the gate to another place . . . with the woods ending there . . . and the fields and the hills stretching down to the river. It's a pleasure when you're walking with feet feeling the ground underneath you. It's a pleasure to go through it.

Janet (*touching his hand lightly*)   Come on, David . . . We'll talk about it in bed.

She turns down the lamps, takes one, and they walk together into the bedroom.

Shooting the Legend

Alan Plater

Shooting the Legend was first performed at the Newcastle
Theatre Royal on 31 August 1995, with the following cast:

Jacky	Tim Healy
Gazza	Trevor Fox
Fiona	Lesley Vickerage
Matt	Dave Whitaker
Barbara	Charlie Hardwick
Kate	Denise Welch
Pat	Libby Davison
Darren	Chris Connell
A whippet	Holly

The Felling Band conducted by Raymond Poole

Directed by Max Roberts
Designed by Perry John Hudson
Musical arrangements by Alan Clark

Editor's Note

This was a joyful experience from start to finish – made possible by Grahame Morris, the then General Manager of the Newcastle Theatre Royal (a receiving house), who took the unprecedented gamble of bankrolling the pre-production costs against box office. Thankfully, it proved no risk at all as the show enjoyed a sell-out run. Playing the Theatre Royal was a great thrill for the cast, many of whom had been taken there as youngsters for their first experience of theatre. This uplifting comedy exemplifies Alan's uncanny ability to write for this large and enthusiastic audience, combining his unique sense of humour with direct local relevance and wry profundity.

Characters

Jacky
Gazza
Matt
Barbara
Kate
Darren
Pat

Band as available

Act One

Lights up on the Bedewell Club, somewhere in uptown Tyneside.

There's a bar, naturally. There are little circular tables and stools. There's a tiny stage area for concerts, with an electronic keyboard, a drumkit, a mike stand and a bingo machine full of table tennis balls. There are double swing doors to the outside world. There's a dartboard on the wall.

The walls are covered with pictures of old Newcastle United football teams, boxing posters, Miners' Strike posters, and pictures of assorted local heroes, past and present, though maybe more past than present.

Jacky *sits at one of the tables, watching a television set mounted behind the bar. He's fortyish and a bit of a throwback. He wears trousers with braces, a collarless shirt, a waistcoat and a traditional flat cap. He's looking at the screen over the top of his* Sporting Life. *The muted sound from the television set tells us he's watching afternoon racing.*

While he's concentrating on the screen, **Gazza** *emerges from a storeroom or cellar behind the bar, carrying a couple of empty beer crates. He's in his twenties, wears jeans, a Newcastle United shirt and a black-and-white Toon Army wig. He exits through the swing doors.*

From the television set we hear the key words: 'And they're off.'

Jacky *leans forward, concentrating.*

Gazza *returns, exits behind the bar in unhurried pursuit of more beer crates.*

Jacky *lowers his newspaper.*

Gazza *re-emerges with more beer crates. He makes his way to the swing doors. He exits.*

Jacky *concentrates a little harder.*

Gazza *returns, without beer crates, and disappears behind the bar for more.*

The race reaches a climax.

Gazza *re-emerges, with more beer crates, in time to hear* **Jacky**'s *reaction to the result.*

Jacky   Bugger, bugger, bugger.

He's pretty calm about it. Throws his Sporting Life *to the floor in gentle annoyance.*

Gazza *exits through the swing doors.*

Jacky   Bugger, bugger, bugger, bugger, bugger, bugger.

He gets up, switches down the sound on the television, as **Gazza** *re-enters.*

Bugger, bugger, bugger, bugger, bugger, bugger.

Gazza *disappears behind the bar.*

Jacky *returns to his seat, still muttering.*

Jacky   Bugger, bugger, bugger, bugger, bugger, bugger.

Gazza *re-emerges, carrying more beer crates.*

Gazza   Twenty-one.

Jacky   Twenty-one what?

Gazza   Twenty-one buggers.

This is the first time either has taken any notice of the other.

Jacky   You keep count?

Gazza   Sometimes. It keeps my mind occupied. Your record's thirty-seven.

He picks up the Sporting Life.

You must have backed the winner then?

Jacky   I did.

Gazza   But you only had a couple of quid on it.

Jacky   How do you know?

Gazza   You said bugger twenty-one times. That means you won but you only had a couple of quid on. When you've only had a pound on, you score over thirty buggers. As a rule.

Jacky   What about when I lose?

Gazza   You generally say shit. Too many times to keep count.

Jacky   You're a man of hidden depths, did you know that?

Gazza   It's what everybody says. Except wor lass. She says my depths are a bit shallow.

He stares at the television screen.

Is that the Queen?

Jacky   Aye, the one on the left.

Gazza   I thought I knew the face. She's the dead spit of my Auntie Mary from Shields.

Jacky   I believe Prince Philip says the same. One is the dead spit of Gazza's Auntie Mary from Shields.

Gazza (*stares at the screen*)   You wouldn't believe the things people wear on their heads, would you?

He exits with the beer crates.

Jacky *switches off the television.*

As **Gazza** *returns, he hesitates in the doorway, staring at something outside in the street.*

Jacky   Have you finished the beer crates?

Gazza   Yes. All done. Fancy a game of darts?

Jacky   There's work to be done, man.

Gazza   I shifted the beer crates.

Jacky   Wash the ashtrays, will you?

Gazza (*startled*)   Wash the ashtrays?

Jacky   Yes. Wash the ashtrays?

Gazza   But it's Wednesday.

Jacky   There's no law says you're not allowed to wash ashtrays on a Wednesday.

Gazza   But I washed them last Thursday, no, Friday.

Jacky   It's environmentally sound to keep your ashtrays clean. It's good for the ozone layer. This is a green club.

Gazza   No it isn't. It's dirty brown.

Jacky   We're going green. It was agreed at last week's committee meeting. We're applying for a grant from the Millennium Fund.

Gazza *has another peep outside the door.* **Jacky** *notices.*

Jacky   What's going on out there?

Gazza   There's a car in the street.

Jacky   That's why we have streets, man. To keep cars in.

Gazza   A Mercedes.

Jacky   It'll be a German tourist, looking for Hadrian's Wall.

Gazza   No. There's a woman getting out.

Jacky   All right. A German *woman* tourist. They have women in Germany. *Damen* and *Herren*.

Gazza   She's coming here. Hey, man, she's a doll, like.

Jacky *gets up, crosses to the door to have a look.*

Jacky   You're right. She *is* a doll.

Gazza   What do you reckon?

Jacky   DHSS?

Gazza   I'm not here.

Jacky   If she's from the DHSS, obviously, nobody's here. Maybe she's come about the VAT.

Gazza   Well, that's no problem 'cause you never pay any, do you?

Jacky *returns to his seat.*

Jacky   Whoever she is, we don't know nothing, right?

Gazza   Never been a problem for me, knowing nothing. Tell you what, I'll get on with them ashtrays.

Gazza *starts collecting up ashtrays.* **Jacky** *picks up his* Sporting Life *and starts reading it.*

The doors swing open. In walks **Fiona**. *She's a slightly indeterminate late thirties, wears shades, and a designer trouser suit or such. She carries a shoulder bag. She'd pass unnoticed at BBC Television Centre or in the Groucho Club, but in this context, she might as well be from the planet Mars. She looks around.*

Fiona   Is this the Bedewell Colliery Welfare and Social Club?

Jacky   That depends on who's asking, pet.

Fiona   I am.

She removes the dark glasses. **Gazza** *stares in awe and wonder.*

Gazza   Ye bugger!

Jacky   Let's have a big of decorum, son. Ladies present.

Gazza (*to* **Fiona**)   Hey, you know who you are, don't you?

Fiona   Yes, I know who I am.

Gazza (*to* **Jacky**)   Hey, you know who this is, don't you?

Jacky *crosses to have a closer look at* **Fiona**.

Jacky   Well, without my proper glasses . . .

Gazza   On the telly . . .

Jacky   Unless you do the racing . . .

Gazza   She doesn't do racing, she does like . . . things . . . about things.

Jacky   Things about things? I'll tell you what, bonny lad, it's good to see that a hundred years of compulsory education for the working classes haven't gone to waste. (*To* **Fiona**.) Things about things?

Fiona   Documentaries.

Jacky (*nods*)   Documentaries. We know about them.

Gazza   That's the one. Documentaries. About things. In . . . er . . . wotsit . . . ?

Fiona   Depth.

Gazza   That's it. Documentaries. About things. In depth. That's what she does. She's famous, like.

Jacky   And you're looking for Hadrian's Wall?

Fiona (*baffled*)   Of course not. I know where Hadrian's Wall is.

Gazza   It's north from here, isn't it? Just before Scotland.

Fiona   I'm looking for the Bedewell Colliery Welfare and Social Club.

Jacky   In that case, you're not lost at all.

Fiona   I didn't say I was lost. At no point in this conversation have I indicated I was lost.

Jacky   Well, we're very glad you're not lost. It puts you in a minority of one down this street but we're very happy for you.

Fiona   I was told to ask for Jacky.

Jacky   That's me, pet.

Fiona   Delighted to meet you.

She offers her hand.

A wary handshake.

Jacky   Each way, I'm sure. And obviously you're very famous, but I'm afraid I don't know your name.

Fiona   I'm . . .

Gazza (*breaks in*)   Everybody knows her name, Jacky, man. She's er . . . er . . . Debbie? . . . Esther? . . . Sue? . . . begins with a J . . .

Fiona   Begins with an F.

Gazza   Well . . . F and J . . . they're quite close.

Fiona   Fiona.

Gazza   Fiona, that's it. I knew I knew it.

Jacky   You didn't know it.

Gazza   I'd have got there.

Fiona   *Fiona's Focus.*

Jacky   Is that right?

Fiona   That's my regular slot on Channel 3.

Jacky   Sounds grand. Pleased to meet you, Fiona.

Fiona *turns to* **Gazza**.

Fiona   And you are?

Gazza   Gazza.

Fiona   Gazza?

Even she's heard of **Gazza**.

Gazza   Not the famous one, like. I'm the unknown one. Gazza, it's short for Gary. I mean, it's longer than Gary actually, but that's what it's short for.

Jacky   He just moved here from Mount Olympus.

Fiona   Well, I'm Fiona.

Gazza   I know. You said.

Another wary handshake.

Jacky   So tell us about your regular slot.

Fiona   I focus in depth on topical issues.

Jacky (*looks around*)   Is the social club a topical issue?

Fiona   Not as such.

Gazza   It'd give the darts team a boost, being on telly, wouldn't it? We're second bottom in Division Nine of the Thursday League.

Fiona (*ignores* **Gazza**)   I want to do a *Fiona's Focus* about the traditions of Tyneside. Using your club as a focus.

Jacky   A focus for your focus?

Fiona   Exactly.

Jacky   What sort of traditions had you in mind?

Fiona   You'll have to tell me that. I only know what I've read about.

Gazza   And seen in in-depth documentaries?

Fiona   Are we talking leek competitions? Whippet racing? Folk singing? Or are they the invention of the heritage industry? Either way, I thought we might peg the whole thing to the Northumberland Plate.

Jacky   The Pitman's Derby?

Fiona   I believe it's upcoming, isn't it?

Gazza   No. It's next Saturday.

Fiona   Will you be there?

Quick exchange of looks between **Jacky** *and* **Gazza**. *Obviously they never go, but they've spotted the possibility of a main chance.*

Jacky   You bet we do. I mean, wild horses wouldn't keep us away from the wild horses.

Gazza   It's the big event of the year. Along with the other big events, like. The tall ships and the first home game of the season and . . .

He stumbles to a halt, unable to think of any other big events.

Jacky   The annual visit of the Royal Shakespeare Company?

Gazza   Sometimes we hire a bus.

Jacky   That's right.

The bus is obviously a new thought.

Gazza   With balloons and cake for the bairns, like.

Jacky   Or a minivan depending on the demand, and the state of the economy.

Fiona   A bus would be brilliant.

Jacky   We haven't actually hired it yet. We tend to be . . . creatures of impulse. Ask us again on Friday.

Fiona   I'm thinking about the visuals, you see.

Jacky   Visuals?

Fiona   We had a BAFTA nomination for our camera work this year.

Gazza   Did you make a speech saying thank you to your mam and dad and Tom Cruise?

Fiona   We didn't actually win. (*Sees the* Sporting Life.) I imagine you'd say, we were beaten a head into second place.

Jacky   You should have objected. Asked for a stewards' inquiry. (*Looks around.*) So where's the cameraman?

Fiona   I do the lot myself. Lighting. Sound. And I operate the camera. Generally hand-held.

Gazza   Hand-held? (*He sniggers.*) That sounds canny.

Jacky   Does that mean, you hold the camera with your hand?

Fiona   Hands. Both of them.

She demonstrates, in mime, how she holds the camera.

Gazza   So that's hand-held?

Fiona   It's a question of style. It's more realistic.

She looks at her watch.

Oh my God, is that the time?

Jacky   We watched the three o'clock race so it must be getting on for half past.

Fiona   I have to call the office.

Jacky   There's a telephone beside the gents.

Fiona   It's all right.

She brings a mobile phone from the depths of the shoulder bag. She taps in a number and listens.

Gazza   I've always fancied one of them.

Fiona   Outrageously expensive. A scam. I did a programme exposing them.

Gazza   I wouldn't buy one from a shop, like.

Fiona (*can't hear anything*)   I'll have to take it outside. Excuse me.

She exits.

The lads stand up in studied politeness. They give the situation a bit of thought, then:

Gazza   What do you reckon?

Jacky   Mad as a hatter.

Gazza   Well, obviously, she's crackers, but she seems nice enough with it.

Jacky   Leeks, whippets and folk songs.

Gazza   But that's what's expected, isn't it?

Jacky   Doesn't she know the leeks won't be ready for another couple of months?

Gazza   Can't stand the taste of leeks. Any sort of onion makes us puke. Me, I like traditional-style Geordie kebabs.

Jacky   And I haven't been to the Northumberland Plate since I was ten. My Uncle Leonard took me. He loved the horses. He'd have been a jockey himself except he had this problem.

Gazza   What was his problem?

Jacky   He weighed eighteen stone.

Gazza   Hey, I didn't mean to drop you in it, about the bus and the balloons for the bairns, all that. It sounded good, though, didn't it?

Jacky   Listen. The thing you've got to remember about all these great Tyneside traditions is they're subject to change. The world changes. The traditions change.

Gazza   Is that right?

Jacky   They're in a constant state of flux.

Gazza   Flux?

Jacky   Flux.

Gazza   Is that like change?

Jacky   Very similar.

Gazza   Got it.

Jacky   So when she starts asking us about the great Tyneside traditions, they can be whatever we want them to be.

Gazza   You mean, make them up, like?

Jacky   They're our traditions.

Gazza   Like my wig.

Jacky   What?

Gazza (*indicates his wig*)   If enough people do it, it becomes a tradition. A Newcastle tradition.

Jacky   Like Royal Ascot.

Gazza   But if I was a Sunderland supporter, it'd be red and white, wouldn't it?

Jacky   Except we don't mention Sunderland in this club. Rule Seventeen.

Gazza   So that's another tradition, isn't it? Not talking about Sunderland.

Jacky   Yes. That's another tradition.

Gazza   There's lots, when you look around, isn't there? Getting pissed on Saturday night. That's another. But you just don't think of them as traditions, do you? They're just the things you do.

Jacky   Yes. Traditions are, very often, just the things you do. It's been like that for thousands of years.

Gazza   That's amazing, man.

Jacky *has a low threshold where* **Gazza**'s *jabbering is concerned. He's just reached it.*

Jacky   Now shut your face, there's a good lad.

Gazza   I'll get on with the ashtrays.

Jacky   Good idea.

Gazza   Hey, that's another tradition, isn't it?

Jacky   Not cleaning the ashtrays.

Gazza   Me talking too much and you telling me to shut up. Been going on a fair while, that one, hasn't it?

Jacky (*gently, wearily*)   Since the beginning of recorded history.

Fiona *returns*.

Fiona   Good.

Jacky   Everything all right in the nation's capital and beating heart of the Empire?

Fiona   Endless meetings about budgets and marketing. Same old shit. It's good to be away from it all.

Gazza *reacts – looks at* **Jacky**.

Gazza   You'd better tell her.

Jacky   What?

Gazza   The club rule.

Jacky   Yes. Right. See. We prefer people to moderate their language when there's ladies present.

Fiona   Women.

Gazza   Either really.

Jacky   It's in the club rules and as steward and minutes secretary, I'd be failing in my duty if I didn't point it out.

Gazza   It's a tradition, like.

Fiona   I'll try to moderate my language.

She sits down at a table, brings out a little tape recorder, sets it down.

May I explain how I do my programmes?

Jacky   Certainly.

Fiona   First I like to talk to people, informally, and get a sense of the story.

Jacky   The story.

Fiona   Then, once I've got a sense of the story, I'll get my camera and we'll start shooting.

Gazza   That'll be for the visuals, right?

Fiona   Yes. The visuals.

Gazza   Thought so.

Fiona   Do you mind if I record our conversation? I'm sure there'll be some gems we can use as voice-over?

Gazza   Over the visuals?

Fiona   Yes. Over the visuals. (*To* **Jacky**.) Happy?

Jacky   Aye. Let's get cracking.

She indicates **Jacky** *should sit at the table with her.* **Jacky** *sits down.* **Fiona** *switches on the recorder.*

Fiona   Interview with Jacky at the Bedewell Club.

Jacky   Bedewell Colliery Welfare and Social Club.

Fiona   There's a good starting-off point. Tell me about the Bedewell Colliery.

Jacky   Bedewell Colliery. That was closed between the wars. In the cellar, where we keep the beer, I can show you the old mine shaft. It's been concreted over, of course. But it's there. It might make a canny visual for your hand-held camera.

Gazza   There's mice in the cellar.

Fiona   I'm not frightened of mice. I did a documentary about them.

Gazza   About their traditions?

Fiona   About vivisection.

Gazza   Is that right? I didn't know mice were religious.

Fiona (*to* **Jacky**)   And are you an ex-miner?

Jacky   Every man in the North-East is an ex-collier. Or an ex-steelworker. Or an ex-shipbuilder. We're all casualties of the basic contradictions of capitalism.

Gazza   I'm an ex-draughtsman. Swan's.

Fiona (*to* **Gazza**)   Could you sit down and join in properly? You're a bit off-mike over there.

Gazza   It never does to be off-mike, does it?

He pulls up a chair and joins them at the table.

Fiona   You know about that?

Gazza   We've got wor own mike over there, look.

Jacky   I use it for calling the bingo. That's where I learned my microphone technique. Yell down the bugger at the top of your voice.

Fiona (*registers a thought*)   Bingo!

Jacky   You've got a lineup?

Fiona   I was thinking . . .

Jacky   . . . it might make a canny visual? When we all come back here after the big race?

Fiona   Possibly. (*Then to* **Gazza**.) Tell me about Swan's.

Gazza   It's where I worked. When I worked. It's a bird sanctuary. You know, Swan's . . .

Fiona   It's a shipyard. Please remember, I work with smartarses every day. Swan's. Is it a shipyard? Or *was* it a shipyard?

She looks to **Jacky** *for an answer.*

Jacky   To be honest, pet, I'm not sure myself. Haven't seen the *Chronicle* today.

Fiona (*to* **Gazza**)   And what do you do now?

Gazza   I help out here mostly. Shifting beer crates. Washing the ashtrays to keep the place green. Miscellaneous duties.

Fiona   So you both work here at the club?

Jacky   That depends who's asking.

Fiona   I'm sorry?

Jacky *reaches out, presses the pause button on the tape recorder.*

Jacky   If you're from the DHSS, we both work here in a purely voluntary capacity.

Fiona   But I'm not from the DHSS.

Jacky *restarts the recorder.*

Jacky   We're renaissance men.

Gazza   Are we?

Fiona   Renaissance men?

Jacky   The capitalists said: we have no further use for you, lads. No more coal. No more steel. No more ships. So that throws you back on your own resources, doesn't it?

Fiona   In what way?

Jacky   That depends on your resources. Me. I run the club. Organise the darts team. Call the bingo. Hear the odd confession. Give absolution.

Fiona   That's extremely versatile.

Jacky   That's what it means, being a renaissance man. Good all-rounder. Like Leonardo. He'd give you the *Mona Lisa* one day, a helicopter the next. *And* he did a very good George Formby impersonation, according to my Uncle Joe.

Fiona (*to* **Gazza**)   And are you a renaissance man too?

Gazza   I don't know. Am I?

Jacky   Tell her what you do here Saturday night.

Gazza   Oh. Is that renaissance? I'm an alternative comedian.

Fiona   Fascinating.

Gazza   A lot of people say that. Fascinating.

Jacky   Alternative comedy. It's the new rock and roll. I heard that on *The Late Show*.

Fiona   Quite so. And how would you define alternative comedy?

Jacky   I'll put it this way. I've heard a lot of comedians in my time, and this bonny lad's alternative to any of them.

Fiona   Could you give me an example of your alternative comedy?

Gazza   You mean a joke, like?

Fiona   Yes please. A joke, like.

Gazza   Well, for example, I could say to you: What's the difference between roast beef and pea soup?

Fiona   What *is* the difference between roast beef and pea soup?

Gazza   You can roast beef.

No reaction. An uneasy silence, then:

Gazza   I mean, we've both heard it before, so we're not likely to laugh.

Fiona   Do your audiences laugh?

Gazza   Not very much. That's how you tell it's alternative.

Jacky   They laugh at your jokes about Gateshead and the Prime Minister.

Gazza   But that's easy.

Fiona   Could you give me an example?

Gazza   It's the same joke. Why do the pigeons fly upside down over Gateshead and the Prime Minister?

Fiona (*getting the idea*)   I don't know. Why do the pigeons fly upside down over Gateshead and the Prime Minister?

Matt *enters in time to deliver the punchline.*

Matt   Because neither of them's worth shitting on.

He is in his thirties. He's heavily laden with Tesco shopping bags. He's a phlegmatic man who accepts everything – fire, flood, tempest – with total equanimity.

(*Sees* **Fiona**.) Sorry, pet. Didn't see you sitting there. (*To* **Jacky** *and* **Gazza**.) Now then, lads. Where do you want the groceries, Jacky? Usual place?

Jacky   Aye, through the back, ta.

Matt *continues his journey into the back.*

Fiona   Another renaissance man?

Jacky   Absolutely.

Gazza   He's a keyboard player.

Jacky   These days, you're either a renaissance man or you're dead.

Matt *returns from the back room, free of his burden. We now see that he's also carrying a baby in a harness strapped to his chest.*

Matt   I'll just get the rest.

He exits.

Fiona   Er . . . was he carrying a baby?

Gazza   Oh aye. Takes it with him everywhere.

Jacky   Keyboard player, barman and house-husband.

Fiona   Another renaissance man?

Jacky   They don't come any more renaissance than that lad.

Matt *returns. This time he's got a few more Tesco bags, plus a carrycot.*

Matt   I'll just get the bairn settled and I'll join you.

He wanders through into the back.

Fiona   Another ex-miner?

Jacky   No. He's redundant from the building trade.

Gazza   He's brilliant at shelves. Do you use shelves?

Fiona   All the time.

Gazza   He's your man.

Matt *returns to the room, now free of all burdens.*

Matt   Hey, it was like a madhouse in the supermarket. And would you believe, no aubergines? Ye bugger.

Jacky   No aubergines? That's what triggered off the French Revolution.

Matt   Is this a private meeting?

Fiona   Please join us.

Matt   Ta.

Matt *sits down.*

Fiona *stops the tape recorder.*

Fiona   My name's –

Matt (*breaks in*)   Fiona, as in *Fiona's Focus*, Channel 3, in-depth documentary series.

Fiona   That's nice.

Matt   Love the programme you did about the mice.

Fiona   Thank you. And you are . . . ?

She starts the tape recorder.

Matt   Matt. As in doormat, but with two t's.

Gazza   She's going to do a *Fiona's Focus* about the Northumberland Plate.

Jacky   But focused on the club.

Gazza   And great Tyneside traditions like leeks and whippets and folk songs and my wig.

Matt   Sounds grand. (*To* **Jacky**.) Special occasion, this, isn't it? We've never had an in-depth documentary made about us, have we?

Jacky   That's true.

Matt   So I think you should take an executive decision to open the bar.

Jacky   Sorry, I'm forgetting my manners. Pints all round, is it?

Fiona   Not for me, thank you. I don't drink beer.

Jacky   What would you like?

Fiona   Perhaps a spritzer?

Jacky   A spritzer?

Gazza   I thought that was a German car.

Matt   White wine and soda water. With ice and a tiny sliver of lime.

Jacky (*to* **Gazza**)   Away you go.

Gazza   Me?

Jacky   While Matt tells Fiona about his life story.

Gazza   Right.

Gazza *crosses to the bar and fixes the drinks.*

Fiona   I'm told you're also a renaissance man.

Matt   I do a lot of things. I'm head of security here. I call myself Group Six-to-Four Against. And I help behind the bar. Play keyboards. Do the shopping. Mind the bairn.

Fiona   What's the baby's name?

Matt   Aneurin.

Fiona   Aneurin?

Jacky   If you have to ask, you wouldn't understand anyway.

Fiona   Have you given up the building trade?

Matt   It's not a trade any more. It's Dodge City. Everybody's a cowboy. I did some work in London in the eighties. Do you want it done properly or do you want it done by Thursday? Always the same answer. Thursday.

Jacky   He worked on Canary Wharf.

Fiona   You did?

Matt   That sums it up. Nobody wants it. Nobody likes it. Nobody can pay for it. They don't make canaries that big.

Gazza *arrives at the table with a tray of drinks: three pints.*

Gazza   The pigeons fly upside down over Canary Wharf.

Jacky   They fly upside down practically everywhere these days. (*Looks at the tray.*) Hey! Where's Fiona's drink?

Gazza   I did the easy ones first. What was it you said?

Matt   A spritzer. I'll see to it.

Matt *gets up, crosses to the bar.*

Gazza (*to* **Fiona**)   I'm sorry. I'm still learning, you see.

Fiona   Learning?

Gazza   How to be a renaissance man.

Fiona   And what about the women?

Gazza   What about them?

Fiona   Are you all married?

Jacky   Oh aye, we're all married.

Fiona   And where are your wives?

Gazza   They're out at work.

Jacky   They'll be back soon.

Gazza   Except wor lass. She's on the late turn.

Fiona *gets the picture.*

Fiona   So what we have here is a major economic and sociological shift.

Jacky   Everywhere you look.

Fiona   The women work. The men stay at home. Exactly the opposite of the industrial tradition.

Matt *delivers* **Fiona**'*s drink.*

Matt   The men wait at table.

Fiona   Thank you very much.

Matt   You're welcome.

Fiona *takes a sip.*

Fiona   Delicious.

Matt   I try to be a craftsman, whatever I do.

He sits down.

Gazza   The women go out to work. The men sit around watching the racing and supping pints. I can handle that.

Jacky   That's chauvinist talk, man.

Gazza   Is it? Good.

Gazza *assumes it's a compliment.*

Matt   See, what you have to do is reclaim yourself.

Fiona   How do you mean?

Matt   The system chucks you out. Tells you you're neither use nor ornament. You've got to prove the system's wrong. You've got to prove to yourself that you can do something.

Fiona   And you three have set about reclaiming yourselves using this club as your focus?

Jacky   I suppose we have really. Organising the darts.

Matt   Serving behind the bar.

Jacky   Calling the bingo.

Gazza   Telling a few jokes.

Jacky   Comforting the sick and the needy.

Matt   Providing care in the community.

Fiona   Could you give me an example?

Jacky   Of what?

Fiona   Care in the community? If you're claiming this club has a social role beyond its walls?

Jacky   Certainly it has. Historically speaking, the miners' welfare was the centre of education, of learning, of debate, of culture. They had lecture halls and libraries.

Fiona   Do you have a library?

Jacky   No. We bootleg the odd video, but that's about it.

Gazza   You could get *Reservoir Dogs* here before it was out on general release.

Matt   But the principle's still alive and well.

Fiona   Is it?

Gazza   Is it?

Jacky   Is it?

Matt   Care in the community? Definitely. (*To* **Fiona**.) That's your Mercedes outside?

Fiona   Yes.

Matt *dips his hand into his pocket. He brings out the decorative logo that normally stands on the car bonnet.*

Matt   I took the liberty of removing that.

He passes it to **Fiona**.

Fiona   Why did you do that?

Matt   A sensible precaution. The kids'll be out of school any minute. If I hadn't taken it, you'd never see it again.

Fiona   Care in the community?

Matt   Meaning, when you're in this community, take care.

Fiona   I see. Thank you.

She slips the logo into her bag.

Jacky   So is this all helping?

Fiona   In what way?

Jacky   With the background for your documentary?

Gazza   Your visuals and your voice-overs?

Fiona   It's excellent.

She gets up, takes a look around the place, framing possible shots with her fingers in the traditional directorial fashion.

The lads watch, intrigued.

I was wondering . . . on Saturday, after the race . . .

Gazza   It's going to be a lovely day for the race.

Matt   What race is that?

Gazza   The human race.

Fiona   When you all come back here, will there be any sort of party?

Jacky   You mean like . . . a community celebration?

Fiona   Something of the sort.

Jacky *looks to the others for support.*

Jacky   More than likely.

Gazza   Saturday night I generally get legless anyway, so that's halfway to a party, isn't it?

Jacky   You're looking for visual possibilities, I take it?

Fiona   Absolutely.

Matt   We could have a bit sing-song, couldn't we?

Gazza   Easily, I should think.

Fiona   What sort of music is it likely to be?

Jacky   I shouldn't bank on traditional Tyneside folk songs.

Fiona   I want to share with the viewing audience, truthfully and honestly, what actually happens here in the club.

Jacky   We'll give you a sample if you like.

Fiona   Really?

Jacky   No problem.

Gazza   Let's do the show right here and now.

Matt   I'll need to plug my organ in. If you'll pardon the expression.

Fiona   I should call the London office.

Brings out her mobile.

Jacky   Again?

Fiona   There's a very important production meeting this afternoon. I've got to be up to speed with what's going on.

Jacky   Well, obviously.

Fiona *exits to make her phone call.*

Matt *watches her go. Conversation continues as they prepare their musical instruments: keyboard, drums, guitar and mike as appropriate.*

Gazza   What do you reckon?

Matt   Seems canny enough. What do *you* think?

Gazza   Mad as a hatter, we thought.

Jacky   Two compromises short of New Labour's manifesto.

Matt   But working in the media, it's bound to get to the brain cells, isn't it? Drinking all them spritzers.

Jacky   She's probably a vegan an' all. Give us an A, somebody.

Matt *plays a note on the keyboard.* **Gazza** *plays a totally different note on the guitar.* **Jacky** *whacks the bass drum.*

Jacky   Perfect.

Fiona *returns, a little preoccupied.*

Gazza   All right, pet? Everything up to speed?

Fiona   Yes, fine, thank you. And I ran your title past them and they adored it.

Gazza   What?

Jacky   No disrespect but we haven't a clue what you're talking about.

Fiona   'A Lovely Day for the Race'.

Gazza   It's not a title. It's a very old joke.

Matt   It's a lovely day for the race. What race is that? The human race. At a rough guess, I'd say late 1930s or early forties. Either Bennett and Williams or Clapham and Dwyer or possibly Harry Mooney and Victor King.

Fiona   No disrespect but I haven't a clue what *he's* talking about.

Matt   Long-forgotten music-hall comedians. It's my chosen specialist subject.

Fiona   Whatever its origins, it'll make a wonderful title for the programme. I love its resonance and ambivalence.

Jacky   Wait till you hear the song. It's got resonance and ambivalence we haven't even opened yet.

He looks at the others.

Are you ready, lads?

Matt   If you can whistle it, I can play it.

Gazza   Ready when you are, Mr Barbirolli.

Jacky (*to* **Fiona**)   Are you sitting comfortably?

Fiona *sits down. She has the tape recorder poised and is framing the shot with her hands.*

Fiona   That's lovely. In your own time.

Jacky   All our time is our own, pet.

Matt   That's the problem.

Jacky   So just imagine it's Saturday night, we've all had a lovely day at the races, we've all backed the winner of the Pitmen's Derby and now we've invested wor winnings in a few pints and a few spritzers and pork scratchings and the place is packed to the doors with happy Geordie punters and this is the song they all want to hear.

Turns to the lads.

Lights!

One of them throws a switch to operate a very basic lighting set-up which illuminates their stage area.

After three. Three!

And they go into a stomping version of 'Mustang Sally'. It's a million miles away from any sort of Tyneside musical tradition. Also, they sing and play very well, with some terrific three-part harmony.

A big finish.

One of the lads switches the lights so they revert to normal. They also reveal **Barbara** *and* **Kate** *in the doorway, back from work.*

Barbara *is* **Jacky**'s *wife. She's a primary school teacher.*

Kate *is* **Matt**'*s wife. She sells fast food at the Eldon Centre and wears a daft uniform of some sort, advertising the product: let's say Clarence's Croissant Emporium.*

Barbara   What the hell is going on here?

Jacky   'Mustang Sally'. By special request.

Gazza   Normally we don't play requests.

Matt   Unless anyone asks for them.

Barbara   Answer the question. What the hell is going on?

Jacky   Research.

Fiona *is part hidden behind the bar, where she's been lining up arty shots of the guys in action.* **Barbara** *and* **Kate** *don't see her immediately, and in any case, she's dodging the domestic flak.* **Barbara** *spots the glasses on the table.*

Barbara   This research didn't take the form of sinking a few pints while you watched the afternoon racing on the telly?

Jacky   That set hasn't been on all afternoon, has it, lads?

Looks to the lads for support.

Gazza   Hardly at all.

Matt   I wanted to watch *Fifteen to One* but we were too busy with the research. In depth.

He crosses to **Kate**, *gives her a kiss.*

I've done the shopping, the bairn's sound asleep in his cot and did you have a nice day at the precinct?

Kate   What the hell is going on?

Barbara   You see, I don't know what came over me, but as I was walking down the street, I had a sudden blind impulse . . .

Gazza   They can't touch you for it. Not if you're a consenting adult . . .

Barbara (*ignores him*)   I popped my head into the betting shop and said: any money to collect for my Jacky? And they said, just a few quid, here you are, hinny.

She produces the money, hands it over to **Jacky**.

Jacky   Ta. And there you are, you see, just a few quid. Not a serious bet, just a little flutter, like. For amusement only.

Gazza   I mean, he was really pissed off he didn't have more on. He said bugger twenty-one times.

Barbara   My husband? Swear? I don't believe it.

Gazza   He was under a lot of stress.

Kate   Drinking and gambling, that's one thing . . .

Matt   It's two things, actually, if you count up . . .

Kate   But 'Mustang Sally', that's another matter entirely. 'Mustang Sally'? On a Wednesday afternoon?

At which point **Fiona** *reveals herself, stepping out from behind the bar.*

Fiona   I'm afraid that's my fault.

Kate   What is it? The Wilson Pickett fan club?

Gazza   He comes from round here, doesn't he? Wilson Pickett?

Jacky   Aye. East Boldon, I think. His brother kept a pork butcher's.

Matt   And his uncle played left-half for Blyth Spartans. Mind you, I'm going back a bit now . . .

Kate   Will all the men kindly haad their gobs!

Jacky   We can take a hint. Best of order, lads.

Then **Barbara** *and* **Kate** *look at* **Fiona** *and do the half-recognition routine.*

Kate   Now hang on, didn't you use to do the weather?

Barbara   Or the news?

Kate   Deep depressions and low fronts? Then you went on to *Nationwide*?

Barbara   No, you did the multiplication bits on *Countdown*.

Fiona   Sorry. Not quite.

Kate   *Hearts of Gold*?

Jacky   Oh howay, you're both educated women.

Barbara   *Gladiators*?

Matt   I'll give you a clue. *Fiona's Focus*.

Gazza   That's not a clue. That's the answer.

Jacky   Fiona's researching for a documentary about the Pitmen's Derby.

Barbara   And out of all the gin joints in all of Tyneside you had to walk into this one.

Kate (*recognising* **Fiona**)   *Fiona's Focus*. Channel 3.

Fiona   For my sins, yes.

Barbara   If you've got sins, you've come to the right place.

Matt   Jacky gives absolution, don't you?

Jacky   Except on Sundays.

Fiona (*to* **Jacky**)   Wouldn't it be a good idea if you introduced me?

Jacky   I'm sorry, pet. This is my wife, Barbara. This is Fiona from the telly.

Barbara   Pleased to meet you.

Fiona   Hi.

Matt   And this is my wife, Kate. This is Fiona from the telly.

Kate   Hi.

Fiona   Pleased to meet you.

Kate   And you're doing a programme about the Pitmen's Derby?

Gazza   Yes. It's a horse race. It's upcoming. On Saturday.

Kate (*to* **Gazza**)   I know what it is, you clown. But why make the programme in the club?

Barbara   You'll never get all the horses in here.

Fiona   Well, it seems to me that what we used to call the working-men's club is a perfect symbol of the changing values and social mores in the North-East.

Gazza (*to* **Barbara** *and* **Kate**)   See? You didn't know that, did you?

Fiona   I see the form of the programme as a series of interviews with ordinary working people. Then we'll go to the races with them. Then we'll come back here for the Saturday night celebrations.

Barbara   All joining in 'Mustang Sally'?

Gazza   And whippets and leeks and folk songs.

Barbara   My word, you have been doing your research, haven't you, pet?

Fiona   I'm a good listener.

Barbara   And he's a good talker. (*To* **Jacky**.) What line of bullshit have you been giving her?

Jacky   No bullshit, honey. Just plain, honest truth.

Kate   God help us.

Barbara *and* **Kate** *look at* **Jacky**. *There's an uneasy silence, broken by:*

Matt I tell you what, Jacky. Why don't we make these lasses a nice cup of tea?

Jacky Hey, that's a grand idea. I mean, they've both done a hard day's work . . .

Matt I got some chocolate digestives when I was out.

Jacky *and* **Matt** *head towards the kitchen, which we assume is behind the bar.*

Gazza *isn't going to be left on his own.*

Gazza I'll give you a hand, shall I?

He follows them out.

The women look at each other.

Fiona Did you mean what you said?

Barbara What about?

Fiona Bullshit.

Barbara Probably. He doesn't mean to talk bullshit but after the first thirty years it gets built into the system, doesn't it? Especially in the male of the species.

Fiona (*to* **Kate**) Is that your opinion too?

Kate Yes. It's less obvious with Matt because he doesn't talk as much as Jacky but when he does talk . . . (*Ponders briefly, then:*) yes, it's mostly bullshit.

Fiona Would you be prepared to talk to me?

Barbara I thought we were.

Fiona On the record.

She produces her tape recorder.

Kate More in-depth research?

Fiona Yes.

Barbara Certainly. Why not?

Fiona *leads them to the table where she talked to the lads earlier.*
Barbara *reacts to the empty glasses.*

Barbara   Look at the state of this table.

Matt *shoots out from the kitchen and races them to the table. It's as if he's been keeping lookout.*

Matt   Sorry about that, ladies. We're a bit short-staffed at the moment.

He clears up the glasses and wipes down the table.

Tea'll be up in a minute.

And out he goes again.

The women sit down at the table. **Fiona** *starts the recorder.*

Fiona   'A Lovely Day for the Race'. Interviews at Bedewell Colliery Welfare and Social Club with Barbara and Kate. (*Then to* **Barbara**.) Barbara, you go out to work. Can you tell me what you do?

Barbara   I teach in a primary school.

Fiona   What do you teach?

Barbara   The national curriculum. Today we had a special project on why it isn't a good idea to try to burn down the school.

Fiona   Do you and Jacky have children?

Barbara   Yes, we've got a daughter. She's away at college.

Fiona *turns to* **Kate**.

Fiona   Kate, you also go out to work. Can you tell me what you do?

Kate   I sell fast food in a shopping precinct. Clarence's Croissants. You can have your choice of thirty-seven exotic fillings but most of them taste like cheese.

Fiona   Have you always done that?

Kate   I've always worked, between pregnancies. I used to stack shelves in a supermarket. Then I saw *Educating Rita* and took an Open University degree.

Fiona   That's wonderful.

Kate   Not bad. And I thought, now I've got a degree, I'll get a job on the check-out. But management said I was over-qualified. So I thought bollocks to being a useful member of society, I'll do something really pointless. Clarence's Croissants. Mind you, there are compensations. In exchange for doing a really stupid job you get to wear a totally moronic uniform.

Barbara   I've seen worse uniforms in the precinct.

Kate   You bet. There's Humpty Dumpty selling ice creams and Daleks selling hot dogs and there was talk they were going to dress the security men like Roman soldiers but it was going to cost too much. So they still look like gondoliers.

Fiona   You said between pregnancies. How many pregnancies have you had?

Kate   Only two but they lasted about five years each. The eldest lad's in the sixth form, and the bairn's through the back with his dad.

Fiona   That's a big gap.

Kate   Aneurin was an afterthought. A lovely one, mind. Me and Matt, we drank too much at New Year and, well, you know how it is. You start playing your old Billie Holiday records and next thing, you find it isn't just the New Year you've let in.

Barbara   My grandma used to have an embroidered sampler over her bed. It said: 'Look not upon the ale when it is Newcastle Brown.'

Fiona   But basically, you're both breadwinners?

Barbara   Underpaid, undervalued and exploited, but yes.

Fiona   How do you feel about that?

Barbara   Do you want an honest answer?

Fiona   Please.

Barbara   Terrific.

Kate   Me too.

Fiona   What about your husbands?

Barbara   How do you mean?

Fiona   How do you feel about them staying at home?

Barbara *and* **Kate** *look at each other, hesitate, then:*

Kate   You're asking us to talk about them behind their backs?

Fiona   Yes please.

Barbara   Easily the best way.

Kate   Well, I'll tell you what I think . . .

But before she can do so, the lads enter. **Matt** *carries a tray with tea, milk, sugar, cups and saucers.* **Jacky** *carries a plate of biscuits.* **Gazza** *hasn't got anything. All three wear aprons. Elegant as hell.*

Matt   Afternoon tea is served.

Jacky   And there's a selection of biscuits.

The lads prepare the table for the women.

Gazza   And there's nothing for me to carry but if there's anything else you require I'll run and fetch it for you.

Barbara   This is perfect, thank you.

Kate   That'll be all.

Fiona   Thank you very much.

A little pause, as the lads realise they're in the way.

Jacky   You want us to go away again?

Barbara   How else can we talk about you behind your backs?

Matt   That's a fair point.

Jacky   Time was women weren't allowed in this bar at all, except on special occasions.

Barbara   Like the invention of the steam engine.

Kate   Things change.

Matt *reacts to the sound of the baby crying.*

Matt   I'll go feed the bairn.

He exits.

Jacky   And I'll go . . .

He tries to think of something.

Barbara (*helpful*)   You could attend to your leeks.

Jacky   Aye. I'll be out the back with my leeks.

He exits.

Gazza   And I'll go attend to my folk songs.

He exits.

The women settle with their tea. **Fiona** *restarts the recorder.*

Fiona   You were telling me how you feel about your husbands staying at home.

Kate   Terrible.

Barbara   Yes.

Kate   And what makes it worse is we *enjoy* going out to work.

Barbara   So there's guilt on top.

Kate   Even if you're doing a lousy job, you get a buzz from being one of the gang that's doing it.

Barbara You get to understand what it feels like to be a man. And they get to understand what it feels like to be a woman. But we've gained something. And they've lost something.

Fiona Dignity?

Barbara Yes. They've lost the dignity of labour, even if it's stupid, pointless, dangerous labour.

Kate They've been shat upon from a great height by a bunch of gangsters in Whitehall.

Barbara We know their names and addresses.

Kate And I know what I'd like to do to them.

Fiona The politicians?

Kate Yes.

Fiona What?

Kate (*matter-of-fact*) I'd line them up and shoot them.

Barbara So it's no wonder the lads sit around here dreaming about things that never happened.

Fiona Sorry? Can you explain that?

Barbara I'll give you an example. I expect Jacky told you there's an old pit shaft in the cellar? But Bedewell Colliery was closed between the wars?

Fiona Yes.

Barbara Well, there *is* a pit shaft. And it *was* closed between the wars. Between the Napoleonic War and the Crimean War. About 150 years ago.

Fiona I see.

Kate Most of the traditions of the Bedewell Colliery Welfare and Social Club have been invented in this bar, under the influence of draught beer.

And **Barbara** *looks hard at* **Fiona**.

Barbara   So why did you come here? There are proper clubs with proper traditions on Tyneside. You might even find a working colliery, if you're very quick on your feet, even if it's just at Beamish Museum.

Fiona   Out of all the gin joints, I walked into this one?

Barbara   Why?

Fiona   It was my dad's old club. He was born down this street. He talked about it for hours on end.

Kate   Nice middle-class white girl in search of her working-class roots?

Fiona   Is there anything wrong with that?

Kate   Oh no, it does you credit.

Barbara   So who was your father?

Fiona *hesitates, then:*

Fiona   Tommy Carter.

Barbara   Tommy Carter!

She starts to laugh.

Kate   Is that the one who –?

Barbara (*breaks in*)   Yes, that's the one.

Kate *starts to laugh.*

Fiona   I'm sorry. What's funny?

Barbara and **Kate** *quieten down a little.*

Barbara   How can I put this? Er . . . do you know of the circumstances in which your father left the area?

Fiona   I expect they were dubious.

Barbara   That's all right then. Yes. They were. He absconded with the Christmas Club money. He'd been on the take from the fruit machines as well. So if he hadn't absconded, he'd have been run out of town anyway.

Kate   Don't get us wrong. He was held in a lot of respect in the area.

Barbara   He got away with it for so long.

Fiona   And I expect he was funny with it?

Kate   Oh yes. He was canny, like.

Barbara   So what happened to him?

Fiona   Would you believe he drifted to the City? Became a financial consultant?

Barbara   Yes. I can believe that very easily.

Fiona   And ten years ago he ran away to Spain with a dolly bird who designs advertising logos and I haven't seen him since. But as you say, he was canny, like. And he loved to talk about this place. He'd say: when they bury me, they'll find the Bedewell Welfare and Social Club lying in my heart.

She ponders this briefly then, professional again, looks at the tape recorder.

The tape's run out.

She removes the tape, looks at it, looks in vain in her shoulder bag, then:

Fiona   I'll have to slip to the car. Do you mind hanging on? I'd like to talk a little more about gender roles?

Barbara   All right by me. This is my personal time.

Fiona   Two minutes.

She gets up, crosses to the main doors, exits.

Barbara (*shouts*)   You can come out now.

Jacky, **Gazza** and **Matt** *emerge.*

Kate (*to* **Matt**)   How's the bairn?

Matt   Full. Sleeping.

Barbara   And we know something you don't know.

Jacky   That's no surprise. It's the eternal mystery of women, isn't it?

Barbara   Fiona's father was Tommy Carter.

Jacky   Never!

Barbara   It's true.

Matt   Ye bugger.

Gazza   Who's Tommy Carter?

Jacky   Ran this place in the sixties. Cleared off down the A1 with all the money, pursued by the local mafia. He shook them off in Darlington.

Matt   He used to tell that joke about the duck.

Jacky   He still appears in the audited accounts as a bad debt.

Kate   What joke about the duck?

Matt   Did you hear about the duck that couldn't get up for down?

Gazza   I don't understand that.

Matt   It's alternative comedy.

Jacky   Where's she gone?

Kate   She ran out of tape.

Jacky   You must have been talking a lot.

Gazza   What have you been saying about us?

Barbara   We said you're all working-class heroes.

Jacky   Like Tommy Carter?

They share a laugh then go quiet as they become aware of **Fiona** *standing in the doorway, silent and stunned.*

Barbara   What's wrong, pet?

Fiona   I went to the car, opened the boot and my camera's gone.

Barbara   At least they left the car.

Matt   Sort of a camcorder, is it?

Fiona   Yes.

Matt   State of the art?

Fiona   Obviously.

Matt   Expensive?

Fiona   Yes. Very.

Matt   This could be man's work.

Gazza   What?

Matt *doesn't answer. He's having a think.*

Barbara (*to* **Fiona**)   Would you like another cup of tea?

Jacky   Or another spritzer?

Fiona*'s mobile rings.*

Kate   That's probably the local lads trying to sell your camera back to you.

Fiona *extends the aerial.*

Fiona   Hi . . . just a minute . . .

She goes outside to take the call.

Jacky   What was that about man's work?

Matt   Mean streets. The Raymond Chandler quote.

Barbara   'Down these mean streets a man must go, a man who is not himself mean.'

Matt   Right. Down these crappy, old, neglected streets a man must go, a man who is not himself crappy, old and neglected. I think I score two out of the three.

He crosses to the door.

Kate   Where do you think you're going?

Matt   Down the street. You keep an eye on the bairn.

Matt *exits, crossing in the doorway with* **Fiona**, *who puts away her mobile, slips it into her pocket and sits down on the nearest stool.*

Barbara   What's wrong, pet? Hang on, I already said that. Is something else wrong?

Jacky   You lost another camera?

Kate   Your dad's come home?

Fiona   They're not extending my contract.

Jacky   The television company?

Fiona   That's why I've been calling the office all afternoon.

Gazza   You said. Important production meetings. You needed to be up to speed.

Fiona   I am now up to speed. I am on my way out. This will be my last programme.

Gazza   Going to be a bit tricky, without a camera.

Matt *pops his head round the door.*

Matt   Don't want to cause any upset, but it looks like they've taken the wheels off your car.

Jacky   At least you'll have no bother with joy-riders.

Nobody laughs.

A silence, then:

Barbara   You've lost your wheels. You've lost your camera. You've lost your job. Welcome back to your roots, pet.

Fade to blackout.

Act Two

Lights up on the club, as before. It's a couple of hours later, and getting dark outside. We hear the occasional police siren and car alarm as Tyneside goes about its nocturnal business.

Those present: **Jacky**, **Barbara**, **Kate** *and* **Fiona**. *They've had a couple of drinks. There are empty glasses on the tables. They've also eaten some takeaway. There are empty cartons lying around, but tidily.*

The atmosphere is quiet, even a touch elegiac, with maybe a sense that they're waiting for something to happen but don't know what.

Fiona Is it always this quiet on a Wednesday?

Barbara The club doesn't open on a Wednesday.

Kate Or a Monday or a Tuesday or a Thursday—

Jacky (*breaks in*) We only open weekends. At the moment. It's a temporary measure. Till the green shoots come along.

Fiona That's the same reason I've been sacked. Downsizing they call it. Till the green shoots come along. I've been downsized.

Kate Is that better than being rationalised? Or shaken out? Or a surplus resource?

Barbara It's in the national interest, pet. Soon we'll all be leaner and fitter and . . .

Kate (*overlapping*) Leaner and fitter and dead.

A silence, then:

Barbara Never mind. The police'll be here soon.

She looks at her watch.

Fiona The police?

Barbara Just routine, madam.

Kate Jacky . . .

Fiona *is baffled.*

What happens now is obviously an old, well-practised ritual – the women's equivalent to the 'Mustang Sally' routine.

Jacky's *job is to work the backing tracks, though from the audience point of view it looks as if he's playing keyboards.*

The sequence could maybe start with a little finger-snapping, then ease into the first of the songs, which is (let's assume for now) a Tamla Motown medley – school of Diana Ross and the Supremes and Martha and the Vandellas. Stuff like 'Baby Love' and 'Jimmy Mack'. Sultry, late-night music.

But before they start in earnest, **Kate** *and* **Barbara** *cross to the door of the club and throw it open to reveal* **Pat**, *in her police uniform. Big moment, this, with a spotlight, yes? And then into a stonking sequence.*

At the end, **Fiona** *applauds. Naturally. Who wouldn't?*

Fiona   That was brilliant.

Barbara   Couldn't agree more.

Pat   Everything all right then?

Jacky   Yes thank you, officer.

Kate (*to* **Fiona**)   Fiona, this is police person Pat.

Barbara   In her black-and-white hat.

Pat   And you must be Fiona from the telly who does the in-depth documentaries?

Fiona   How do you know that?

Pat   All part of the job, madam.

Fiona   Is it on the national computer?

Pat   No. I met a feller outside and he told me.

She crosses to the door.

Have to be off. There's a crime wave to get on with. See you later, fans.

Jacky   Aye, see you later, pet.

Barbara   Be careful out there.

Kate   Mind how you go.

And away she goes.

They settle down in their places again. Maybe **Jacky** *brings them another round of drinks.*

Fiona   She's very talented.

Kate   Aren't we all?

Fiona   Isn't it a bit of a waste, her being in the police?

Barbara   At least she's in work.

Kate   Anyway, she's family.

Fiona   Oh, I see.

Kate   Scratch anybody on Tyneside, you'll find family.

Jacky   If we're talking about families . . . do you know what always baffled me when I was little?

Barbara   Sex?

Jacky   That still baffles me.

Barbara   I've noticed.

Jacky   I had an Uncle Anty.

Kate   Oh, it's Uncles time.

Jacky   His name was Anthony but they called him Anty for short. So he was Uncle Anty. I could never understand how he could be an uncle and an auntie at the same time.

Barbara   Is there a point to this story? Or are you making a bid to be the Heritage Minister?

Jacky   It's about unemployment. Uncle Anty used to tell this story about *his* Uncle George, who went on the Jarrow Crusade.

Fiona   The Jarrow Crusade? In the thirties, right?

Kate   Protest march. Nineteen thirty-six. The people in Jarrow thought sixty-eight per cent unemployment was a bit too much in the way of downsizing.

Jacky   They'd only gone a couple of miles and Uncle George starts talking to the bloke next to him. He discovers this feller feels so strongly about the situation he's given up his job to join the crusade. So just as they're passing Boldon Colliery, Uncle George turns back, gets this feller's job, saves his wages and eventually becomes the greatest moneylender in the whole of the North-East.

Barbara   My dad used to tell that story. About his Uncle Jim.

Fiona   My dad used to tell it about his Uncle Richard.

Kate   My Uncle Henry was a prisoner of war in the desert but only for a week.

Barbara   For a week?

Kate   He was a pitman from Percy Main. So they set him and his mates on digging trenches. Suddenly they were surrounded by German troops, capturing that bit of the desert. So the lads kept their heads down, hid in the trench, till the Germans moved on. Then a week later the British troops came back and recaptured that bit of the desert. The lads just kept on digging the whole time except when the bullets were flying. After the war Uncle Henry wrote to Churchill to see if he was entitled to any extra money on account of being a prisoner of war for a week but he never heard anything.

Jacky   Churchill must have found out he was a pitman.

Barbara   My Auntie Bella knew a woman in Gateshead who castrated her husband.

Kate   Well, that's Gateshead for you.

Jacky   You never told me that.

Barbara   I didn't want to make you nervous.

Fiona   Is it true?

Barbara   According to my Auntie Bella. He was a right sod from all accounts. Used to get pissed and abuse the kids and wallop his wife. So one Saturday night he came home drunk, so she got the carving knife and cut it off.

Kate   What did she do with it? Cut it in three halves and hoy it down the well?

Jacky   Do you mind?

The women are enjoying the story more than **Jacky**.

Barbara   My Auntie Bella didn't say. Might have given it to the dog for all I know.

Fiona   What happened to the woman?

Barbara   The feller died. The woman was taken to court. The judge said there were extenuating circumstances and let her off prison, but she was bound over to keep the peace.

They laugh.

Fiona   Are they true?

Jacky   What?

Fiona   All these stories?

Jacky   If we want to believe them, they're true.

Kate   Dreams, mostly.

Barbara   We are such stuff as dreams are made on and our little lives are rounded with a giro cheque.

Kate *looks towards the door.*

Kate   What are the lads up to?

Barbara   Did they say where they were going?

Jacky   Men's work, I think.

Kate   God help us.

Fiona   Didn't Matt say something about mean streets?

Kate   Yes, but just because he says things, it doesn't mean you should take any notice.

Jacky   Another beer, anyone?

Barbara   Not for me, pet.

Kate   Nor me.

Jacky (*to* **Fiona**)   Spritzer?

Fiona   No thank you.

Jacky *clears away the food cartons. Then he pulls himself another pint. As he's doing so,* **Matt** *enters.*

Matt (*looks around*)   You're all still here?

Kate   Looks like it. Where have you been?

Matt   Wait there.

He exits. Then returns almost immediately with **Darren**, *who's seventeen, dressed in whatever uniform is favoured by his age group – postmodernist-punk-gothic-grunge or whatever.* **Darren** *has* **Fiona**'s *camera with him.*

Right. That's Fiona. (*Indicates* **Fiona**.) Give her the camera back and tell her you're sorry.

Darren *crosses to* **Fiona** *and returns the camera.*

Darren   I'm sorry.

Darren *is a bit surly and mumbly.* **Matt** *wants more than this.*

Matt   Try harder. Tell her you're very sorry.

Darren   All right. I'm *very* sorry.

Matt   That's better.

Fiona (*accepting the camera*)   Thank you.

Matt   Good. Now I'll introduce you. Fiona. This is our son, Darren.

Darren   Hi, Fiona.

Fiona   Hi, Darren.

Kate   It was my idea to call him Darren.

Darren   She didn't know any better.

Kate   It was before I'd done the Open University course and become sophisticated.

Then she turns on **Darren**.

And what the hell do you think you were doing with that camera?

Darren   I wasn't doing anything with it. I was sitting at home, looking at it.

Kate   And how did you get it home?

Darren   I carried it there. Obviously. Cameras don't have legs.

Kate   You stole it. You broke into Fiona's car and stole it.

Darren   No. I didn't break in.

Matt   I've done a full reconstruction. It was a couple of his mates broke in. They're both doing Petty Larceny at A level.

Barbara   Two of your mates opened the boot?

Darren   Yes. It was really neat, the way they did it.

Jacky   I think I know their names, don't I?

Matt   The usual suspects.

Jacky   Brothers. They did the betting shop last year?

Matt   That's right.

Jacky   Canny lads, both of them. I know their uncle.

Kate   All right. These canny lads open the boot and you just happened to be passing?

Darren   Yes.

Kate   And you said: Let me take care of that camera and I'll make sure it's returned to its rightful owner?

Darren   No. I said: I'll take that home and check it over for you. They all know I'm the film and video expert. I often check things for them. You wouldn't believe the way people neglect their cameras.

Kate   And when you'd checked it over, what were you planning to do next?

Darren *hesitates, then:*

Darren   I was going to keep it.

Matt   I should point out that my son has never stolen anything in his life and has no previous convictions.

Jacky   I can vouch for that.

Darren (*to* **Fiona**)   I mean, it's not *your* camera, is it?

Fiona   It belongs to the company.

Darren   And they're well insured, I bet.

Fiona   Yes.

Darren   So it wouldn't have been a crime against the person. It would have been a crime against the system. And we're all against the system, aren't we?

Matt   He's good, isn't he? You've got to admit, he's good.

Jacky   Oh aye, he's a credit to his father.

Fiona   And you're an expert on cameras?

Darren   You bet.

Matt   You wanted one for Christmas, didn't you?

Kate   And we couldn't afford the one he wanted.

Fiona   This is the one you wanted?

Darren   Obviously. That's why I was going to hang on to it.

Fiona   For making home movies?

Darren   We're not talking home movies, pet. We're talking Hollywood.

Fiona (*flatly*)   Hollywood?

The sound of a van drawing up outside and the slamming of its door. **Jacky** *recognises the sound.*

Jacky   There's a coincidence.

Kate   Where?

Jacky   Darren mentions Hollywood and here comes the star of tomorrow.

Gazza *enters, carrying a huge newspaper parcel.*

Gazza   Hello, folks.

He crosses to **Fiona**.

Those are for you. (*Sees camera.*) You got your camera back then?

Fiona   Yes.

Gazza   That's grand. Where was it?

Fiona   Darren was giving it a five-thousand-mile service.

She takes the parcel and nurses it for the moment, awaiting further instructions.

Gazza *registers* **Darren**'s *presence.*

Gazza   Hi, kid.

Darren   Hi, sucker.

Gazza   What was that about Hollywood?

Darren   Plans for the future.

Gazza   Who's going to Hollywood?

Darren   Me.

Gazza   That's great, man.

He turns to **Jacky**.

Is it all right if I hang on to the van? I've got another couple of calls to make.

Jacky   That's fine.

Kate   Just a minute. Never mind your forward travel arrangements. My son has just gone out of his mind and announced he's going to Hollywood.

Matt   It sometimes happens in a crowded room. Two things going on at once. I've noticed that. Especially at New Year.

Barbara   When are you planning to go to Hollywood, pet?

Darren   Well, obviously not straightaway. Don't worry. I'm going to finish my A levels first.

And he suddenly realises the room is looking at him. He's been caught out and he's on the defensive.

It's all right for you lot, all staring at me. You've all got wacky things going on in your head, haven't you? Once you've discovered you're not good enough to play football for Newcastle United. That's dream number one down the tubes. So what's dream number two?

He focuses on **Jacky**.

Come on, own up. What's yours? Political, isn't it, comrade? Changing the world?

Jacky   Obviously. I'm going to create a social democratic paradise with full employment, where men and women can live in peace and harmony. To each according to their needs, from each according to their capabilities. Starting from the Bedewell Colliery Welfare and Social Club and working outwards. That's my dream.

Barbara   Might take a week or two, honey.

Jacky   Obviously, it's long-term.

Darren *focuses on* **Gazza**.

Darren   And what about you?

Gazza   Everybody knows about me, man.

Darren   The greatest undiscovered alternative comedian this side of the Byker Wall?

Gazza   Sort of.

Darren   Tell us an alternative joke. Make us laugh.

Gazza   Right.

He concentrates, then:

I'm working this club in Gateshead and I said John Major's got a face like a sheep's arsehole and this feller comes up out of the audience and smacks me in the gob. So I says to him: You must be the only Tory in Gateshead. And he says to me: Wrong, kiddar, I'm the only shepherd in Gateshead.

The joke is received with total silence on stage.

Barbara   Coruscating satire.

Gazza   Thanks, Barbara.

Darren   So that only leaves my dad.

He focuses on **Matt**.

What's your dream, Dad?

Matt   I'd like to work at my trade and be a good craftsman.

Kate   Dreams don't come much crazier than that.

Barbara   Easily the daftest yet.

Matt   I know. I wake up every day and then I realise I've woken up.

Jacky   All right. You've put the three of us through the mangle. So what about you? What's your dream, son?

Darren   I'm going to be Quentin Tarantino.

Fiona   Quentin Tarantino?

Gazza   Who's he?

Jacky   Left-sided midfield player. AC Milan.

Darren   The world's greatest film director.

Fiona   You think so?

Darren   You probably prefer the Europeans. What are you? A Fellini freak?

Gazza *heads for the door.*

Gazza   I don't know what anybody's talking about so I might as well be on my way.

Fiona   Before you go . . . am I supposed to unwrap this?

Gazza   It's the best way to find out what's inside.

Fiona *unwraps the parcel. She discovers a bunch of leeks.*

Gazza   You said you wanted some leeks.

Jacky   Where did you get those?

Gazza   I went to see my granda at his allotment.

Jacky   His leeks won't be ready for a couple of months at least.

Gazza   I know. We got these at Safeway's.

Jacky   A traditional Geordie supermarket.

Gazza   My granda marked my card. These'll look all right, he said. Apparently they're grown under simulated artificial conditions in Bulgaria. But they're not bad. As long as you don't eat them, like. Won't be long.

He exits.

Kate   Where's he off to now?

Jacky   I think he's picking up some jokes from a friend.

Barbara   He's probably got an appointment in a pub with an Englishman, an Irishman and a Scotsman.

Their attention reverts to **Darren**.

Jacky   So what are we going to do about Quentin Tarantino?

Matt   We don't have to do anything about him, do we? That's always been my approach.

Darren   I nicked a camera. I returned it to the owner. Case closed.

Fiona   But it isn't that simple, is it?

Darren   I thought it was.

Fiona   I want to know more.

Darren   What about?

Fiona   About you.

Darren   What is there to know?

Fiona   How come a lad like you decides he wants to be a world-famous film director?

Darren   Mainly 'cause I'm no good at football.

Matt   That's true. School second eleven. Substitute. He's a canny lad but.

Darren   What's the point in getting kicked for fun when the rest of your life you're going to get kicked for real?

Then he turns to **Fiona**.

And what do you mean? A lad like me.

Fiona (*a bit shuffly*)   Well, in some ways, with respect, and with the best will in the world, you're . . . a little . . . disadvantaged.

Matt   Disadvantaged? No, I wouldn't say that. He sprained his ankle last year but . . .

Jacky (*breaks in*)   With respect, and with the best will in the world, she means you're a bit common.

Darren   Well, I am.

Barbara   You speak with a funny accent.

Jacky   What they used to call the proletariat.

Kate   Look. Can I just make a point about my common and disadvantaged son? He has never been neglected. And he has never gone without food, shelter or affection.

Darren   That's true. My mam and dad are terrific.

Matt   Are we? That's nice.

Fiona   I didn't mean to be offensive.

Barbara   None taken, I'm sure.

Fiona   All I'm saying is that Los Angeles is full of people who want to be Quentin Tarantino. Only one in a hundred thousand ever makes it. So starting from Tyneside, the odds against are astronomical.

Darren   And all I'm saying is the odds against me are no worse than the odds against Jacky changing the world, or Gazza becoming a star, or my dad getting a decent job at his trade. We're all crazy anyway. So I might as well be really crazy. And Ridley Scott's from Whitley Bay, so there.

Matt   He gets better all the time, doesn't he?

Darren *focuses on* **Fiona**.

Darren   How did *you* do it?

Fiona   How did I do what?

Darren   How did you come to wind up making documentaries about common people like us? Instead of common people like us making documentaries about people like you?

Jacky   Come on, son, be fair. Fiona's been made redundant the same as the rest of us.

Barbara   But she had to be there in the first place so she could be downsized.

Darren   It's a simple question. How did you first get into the television business?

Fiona (*again a bit shuffly*)   Well . . . I started at the BBC and then moved into the independent sector.

Darren   And how did you get into the BBC?

Fiona   I joined the BBC as a researcher when I left Oxford.

Jacky   Oxford?

Barbara   Ancient university town in the south of England.

Kate   I've seen them in the Boat Race.

Barbara   They wear blue. Dark blue. Light blue. One of the two.

Matt   Oxford United's most famous player was Ron Atkinson. I'd say that speaks for itself.

Darren   What did you study at Oxford? Media studies, something like that?

Fiona   No. PPE.

Kate   PPE?

Barbara   Philosophy, Politics and Economics.

Matt   Is that right?

Fiona   Yes.

Matt   I always thought PPE was a private health scheme.

Jacky   No, you're getting confused with the Public Sector Borrowing Requirement.

Matt   I'm *always* getting those two mixed up.

Fiona   Anyway, I know what you're all thinking.

Matt   I wasn't thinking anything. (*To* **Kate**.) Were you thinking anything?

Kate   Very little.

Jacky   What are we thinking, pet?

Fiona   You're thinking I only got my job in the media because I was in a privileged position. Private school education, closed scholarship to Oxford, Oxford to the BBC. That's the bottom line, right?

She challenges the room.

Barbara   I wasn't thinking that. (*To* **Kate**.) Were you?

Kate   No, I wasn't thinking that. (*To* **Matt**.) Were you?

Matt   No. I was trying to think of another decent footballer that played for Oxford United, but I couldn't.

Jacky   But I was thinking *exactly* that. Fiona got her cosy job in the media because of middle-class power and privilege. But then, I'm a card-carrying proletarian. You'd expect me to think that. (*To* **Darren**.) How does it look to the younger generation?

Darren   Exactly the same. I agree with you, Jacky.

Fiona   And I agree with both of you.

Jacky   You do?

Fiona   That's how the system operates.

Jacky   But this is a real spicy example, isn't it?

Barbara   How do you mean?

Jacky   Well, ask yourself. How did Fiona's dad win his position of power and influence.

Matt   Don't know. Give in.

Barbara   He ran off with the Christmas Club money.

Jacky   Right.

Kate   You've got to admit, it's clever.

Barbara   I mean, with respect and with the best will in the world, Tommy Carter, your old man, was a Thatcherite years before the woman had even invented herself.

Fiona   I know that better than anyone.

Kate   The Wicked Witch of the South.

Darren   But we're all Thatcherites, aren't we?

Jacky   Speak for yourself.

Darren   I see the kids breaking into a car boot. There's a nice camera lying there. I see it. The main chance. Maybe the only chance I'll ever get. So I take it. Stand on my own feet. Go for it. All that crap. That's it, isn't it? Competitive. Lean. Fit. Stand on your own feet. And if you stand on other people's that's their fault for being in the way. That's the bottom line. That's Thatcherism. That's the national curriculum.

Jacky   You sound as if you believe it.

Darren   What choice have I got?

Jacky   Change the curriculum?

Darren   You've been trying all your life and what have you achieved?

Jacky   The game's not over yet. It could still go to extra-time and penalties.

Darren   With respect and with the best will in the world, bollocks.

Kate   It's terrible, the words they pick up in the playground. I blame Channel 4.

Darren   Look at my mother.

Kate   Oh, is it my turn now?

Darren   You do an Open University degree and you're brilliant and honestly I'm really really proud of you but what's your reward? Cheap labour selling fast food dressed up like the fairy on the Christmas tree.

Barbara   So we got it wrong. We made a mess. We failed. We ruined your life. What are you going to do about it?

Darren   I'm going to look after number one. I'm going to try to be Quentin Tarantino and if I have to steal a camera to do it, that's what I'll do. I'll try not to hurt anyone and I won't wind up hustling drugs but apart from that, all bets are off. The woman was right. There's no such thing as society. There was, once upon a time. But you let the Wicked Witch crap all over it. Game over. Sorry, comrades.

He falls silent. So do the others. Out of the silence:

Barbara   Did you get all that down?

This to **Fiona***, who's been making notes.*

Fiona   Yes.

Kate   You're getting plenty of material for your documentary. You should go out with a bang.

Fiona   No. Not me.

Kate   What?

Fiona *gets up, picks up the camera, crosses to* **Darren**.

Fiona   Here.

Darren   What?

Fiona   You make the programme. Quentin.

Darren   What programme?

Fiona   Mine. 'A Lovely Day for the Race'. A celebration of the great traditions of the North-East as the common people prepare for the excitement of the Northumberland Plate.

Darren   Is that what it's supposed to be about?

Fiona   That's what I sold to my producer.

Matt   Why do you think Gazza brought the leeks?

The leeks are on the table, more or less where **Fiona** *dumped them.*

Darren   And you want me to make the programme?

Fiona   I'm offering you my position of privilege.

Darren   I see. (*Hesitates, then:*) Right then.

Darren *takes the camera. He tries various positions in the club, checking possible shots through the viewfinder. He's a little wary and nervous but beneath it all, he knows what he is doing.*

As he's doing this, **Jacky** *crosses to the bar.*

Jacky   Drinks anyone?

Barbara   Who's paying?

Fiona   The company. I have a programme budget. Get in quick while stocks last.

Barbara   Right. Large gin and tonic please, pet.

Kate   Same for me, please, Jacky.

Fiona   And for me.

Jacky   Matt?

Matt   Aye, I'll have another pint. (*To* **Kate**.) I'll just check the bairn's all right.

Matt *crosses to the door behind the bar.*

Darren   Can you just do that again, Dad?

Matt   Do what again?

Darren   That move from where you were to where you are now?

Matt   What for?

Darren   So I can see what it looks like on camera.

Matt   From where I was to where I am. Right.

He returns to his original position.

Do you want the Robert De Niro walk?

Darren   Just act natural.

Kate   Donald Duck.

Matt   Shall I start now?

Darren   It's not a big deal. Just do it.

Matt   I'll have a pint please, Jacky. (*To* **Kate**.) I'll just check the bairn's all right.

He repeats the move, a bit self-consciously. He exits, then pops his head around the door.

Was that all right?

Darren   Yes, fine.

Matt   Did you film it?

Darren   No. I'm just working out the framing of my opening shot.

Matt   Like a rehearsal?

Darren   Yes. Like a rehearsal.

Matt   Good. I'll just check the bairn's all right.

This time he goes.

Jacky *crosses to the table with drinks for the women.*

Jacky   He's got a funny walk, your Matt, hasn't he?

Barbara   I've seen funnier.

He distributes the drinks.

Fiona   Thank you.

Kate   Thanks, pet.

Barbara (*a toast*)   Here's to the budget.

Kate   And the company that made it possible.

Fiona   May they rot in hell.

Barbara   You're a quick learner.

Darren   Jacky. Can you switch the light on over the dartboard?

Jacky   Did you want a game?

Darren   No. I need some light in that bit of the frame.

Jacky   You shall have some light in that bit of the frame. Let there be light.

He crosses to the dartboard, switches on the overhead light.

And there was light. And on the seventh day he rested on account of being given compulsory redundancy.

Darren (*oblivious to all around him*)   I'm going to have to cheat these tables a bit.

He locks off the camera which, let's assume, is on a tripod.

Kate   Is that the way Tarantino talks? All that stuff about framing shots and cheating tables.

Fiona   I've never met Quentin Tarantino.

Darren *moves around the room, rearranging furniture in the apparently meaningless way familiar to anyone who's watched film directors in action.*

Fiona   I once interviewed Peter Greenaway.

Jacky   Greenaway? He's a jockey.

Barbara   He's a film director.

Jacky   Well, if you ever interview the jockey, you can tell him, he owes me a lot of money. (*A look from* **Barbara**.) Well, a couple of quid.

Matt *emerges from the back room.*

Matt   I have an announcement to make. The bairn is sleeping like a baby.

He finds himself face to face with **Darren**.

Where would you like me to stand?

Darren   Anywhere you like. Just act natural.

Matt   Act natural. I've never found that easy.

Jacky   Here, man. Drink that.

He gives him his pint.

Matt   Now that's easy.

He sits down with his pint.

The main door opens and **Gazza** *enters carrying a load of paper: A3 size. He crosses to* **Fiona** *and presents her with the pile.*

Gazza   I've spent some money but I've got a receipt.

Barbara   Ask her nicely, she might find it in the budget.

Kate   There might be enough over for a drink.

Gazza   Great. I'll have a pint please, Jacky.

Fiona   What's this?

Gazza   Folk songs.

Fiona   Folk songs?

Gazza   You said you wanted folk songs so I went to the library and said: Have you got any folk songs? They've got hundreds.

Fiona   So I see.

Gazza   But they're in the reference library. That means you're not allowed to take them out.

Fiona   Yes. I know how reference libraries work.

Gazza   But you can photocopy them. There's the receipt. Fourteen pounds and twenty-five pee.

He gives her the receipt.

Fiona   Thank you.

She looks at the receipt then dips into her bag and finds the money.

Gazza   Have a look through them, like, and if there's one that takes your fancy, we can learn it.

Matt *wanders over to look at the music.*

Fiona *gives* **Gazza** *his money.*

Fiona   Fifteen pounds. Keep the change.

Gazza   Thank you, pet.

Fiona *looks through the music, passing it to* **Matt**, *page by page.*

Fiona   Do you know any of these?

Gazza   Me? No, I don't mess with that stuff, like. It's mostly finger-in-your-ear music, isn't it?

Barbara   Finger-in-your-ear?

Gazza   You know.

He sticks his finger in his ear, in a parody of the great Ewan MacColl, and improvises.

(*Sings.*)

Oh come all ye good colliers
A song I'll sing to you
Of how they closed your collieries down
In nineteen ninety-two.

They closed some more in ninety-three
They only kept the best
And then in nineteen ninety-four
They closed the bloody rest.

End of the song. Nobody's very impressed.

Jacky   It's political satire.

Barbara   Coruscating.

Gazza   No. I made it up as I went along.

Matt *finds some music he recognises.*

Matt   I know this one. And this one.

Fiona   See? Matt knows some of these songs.

Gazza   But he's older than I am.

Barbara   I think the general idea is that folk songs are handed down by word of mouth, from generation to generation. The folk tradition.

Gazza   Folk songs are songs that folk sing, you mean? Like 'There's Only One Peter Beardsley'?

Matt *takes some of the music across to the keyboard, bumping into* **Darren** *who's still rearranging the furniture.*

Matt   Will it spoil your framing if I sit over here for a bit?

Darren   That's all right. It's the external lighting that's the problem.

Matt *sits down at the keyboard. He tries a few pieces of the music, quietly, ad lib, while the rest of the room goes about its business.*

Gazza *is intrigued by* **Darren***, who is on his way back to look through the camera viewfinder.*

Gazza   What you doing, son?

Darren   Setting up the master shot.

Gazza   It's time somebody did.

He turns to **Jacky***.*

Do you know what he's on about?

Jacky   He's off to Hollywood to be Quentin Tarantino.

Gazza   That's all right then.

Darren   I need to do something about the outside lighting.

Jacky   We've been complaining about that for years. People leaving the club, they're always falling over.

Barbara   We've written to the council.

Jacky   And the European Court of Justice.

Kate   You'd be better off writing to Jimmy Savile.

There's the sound of a car alarm from outside as **Darren** *exits.*

Meanwhile, **Matt** *discovers a song that he knows.*

Matt   Hey, I know this one.

Gazza   What one's that?

Matt   'Wor Nanny's a Mazer'.

Jacky   Why, everybody knows that.

Gazza   I don't.

Jacky   Course you do.

Gazza   Do I?

Matt *and* **Jacky** *go into a quick burst – the opening bars – in their broadest Geordie accents.*

Matt/Jacky (*playing and singing*)

Wor Nanny and me made up wor minds
To gan and take the train
To gan to the toon to buy some claes
For wor little Billy and Jane
But when we got to Rowlands Gill
The mornin' train was gone
And there wasn't another one gannin' that way
Till seventeen minutes to one . . .

At which point, approximately, they're interrupted, simultaneously, by **Fiona** *and* **Darren**, *as he returns.*

Fiona   Excuse me.

Darren   Excuse me.

Fiona   Sorry.

Darren   Sorry.

Fiona   You go first.

Darren   Oh no, you go first, you're the visitor.

Fiona (*to* **Jacky** *and* **Matt**)   I just wanted to say that I enjoyed that very much and I didn't understand a single solitary word.

Kate *crosses to the musical group.*

Kate   We'll sing it with subtitles.

Fiona   Thank you. I'd appreciate that.

Barbara   It's wonderful, isn't it? There are still forms of the English language that need translation.

Kate   Like Prime Minister's Question Time.

Then they realise **Darren** *is waiting for them to finish.*

Matt   Your turn, son.

Darren   I'm ready to do the opening shot.

Kate   Well, you get on with your shooting and we'll get on with our singing.

Darren   But that wasn't the way I saw it.

Fiona   How did you see it?

Darren   Well, I thought an establishing shot with my dad and Gazza playing darts, and Jacky serving behind the bar.

Jacky   That's a bit stereotypical, isn't it?

Barbara   And what about the women?

Darren   Ah. Yes. Well. See. I thought you could be sitting at the table there, sort of drinking and chatting.

Kate   What? Talking about babies?

Barbara   I could slip and get my knitting if you like.

Darren   Well, no, then, just sit there and watch the darts.

Darren *has said the wrong thing!*

Kate (*to* **Darren**)   Where have you been all your life?

Darren   Well, sort of . . . around.

Kate   We no longer live in a world where the men play darts and the women watch.

Jacky *becomes aware of a draught where* **Darren** *has left the outside door ajar.*

Jacky   And we don't live in a world where people leave doors open.

He closes the door.

Darren   I need that open for the shot, man. I get the light from outside shining across the floor. It's really interesting.

Darren *crosses to the door, opens it again.*

Jacky   All right. We'll give way on the door. You give way on the song.

Darren   What?

Matt   I can see this going to arbitration.

Kate (*to* **Fiona**)   How would you deal with a situation like this?

Fiona   The classic rule of documentary is tell the truth.

Kate   There you are, see? Tell the truth.

Barbara   And the truth is we're going to have a bit sing.

Darren *has another look through his viewfinder.*

Darren   Well, where are you going to stand?

Barbara   How the hell do we know?

Gazza   We'll move about, won't we?

Jacky   We might even dance.

Kate   Or jump up and down.

Barbara   You can never tell what might happen when the word's upon us.

Darren   All right. Go ahead and sing. Jump about if you want to. Just make sure you don't get between the camera and the door.

He indicates the area he wants them to keep clear of.

Jacky   Is that because it's really interesting the way the light shines on the floor?

Darren   That's right. (*He appeals to* **Fiona**.) You have a look. You tell them.

Fiona *crosses to the camera. She has a look. There's a sense that she's now in alliance with* **Darren**.

Fiona   Yes. It's really interesting the way the outside light shines on the floor.

Darren   See? Now do you believe me?

Fiona   Where would you like me to sit, Darren?

Darren *indicates a chair.*

Darren   You sit there and listen to the music.

Matt   Are we ready yet?

Darren   When I call action.

Gazza   Ready when you are, Mr de Mille.

Darren   All right. Camera running. And action!

Darren *watches through the camera as the gang do the song.*

Matt *starts playing.*

Before they start singing, **Barbara** *speaks to* **Fiona** *and through her, in effect, to the audience. She's a bit like a BBC person introducing a Promenade concert.* **Matt** *busks on the keyboard as* **Barbara** *speaks.*

Barbara   This is a politically incorrect nineteenth-century music-hall song. The singer is a small man called Bob who is married to a woman called Nan or, in the vernacular, Nanny. Nan is a large woman or, as we now prefer to say, dimensionally challenged. The opening stanza tells how Bob and Nan plan to go shopping but miss their train and adjourn to a public house.

And they sing the song, probably passing the words, relay fashion, from one to another (to be figured out in rehearsal). Except they sing it fast, and get faster all the time.

They sing.

Wor Nanny and me made up wor minds
To gan and take the train
To gan to the toon to buy some claes
For wor little Billy and Jane
But when we got to Rowlands Gill
The mornin' train was gone
And there wasn't another one gannin' that way
Till seventeen minutes to one
Says I to wor Nan, it's a long way to gan

And I saw by her face she was vexed
Says I, nivvor mind we have plenty of time
We'll stop and gan on with the next
She got a bit smile when I spoke up and said
There's a public house along here
We'll gan alang there and get worselves warm
With a gill of the best bitter beer
But Nan was sae stout and I knew she'd not walk
And she didn't seem willing to try
When I think of the trouble I'd with her that day
I'd like to burst out and cry

Into the chorus and naturally the aim should be to get the audience joining in. **Fiona** *might help in this.*

And aye wor Nanny's a mazer
And a mazer she'll remain
As lang as I live I'll nivvor forget
The day we lost the train.

Matt *vamps.* **Kate** *explains.*

Kate   In the second stanza, Bob, the man of limited growth, explains how his wife, the amazing Nanny, has a little too much to drink.

And they sing.

So down we went to the public house
And when we got through the door
She says, we'll gan to the parlour end
I've nivvor been there afore
So in we went and teuk wor seats
And afore I rang the bell
I asked her what she was gannin' tae hev
And she says, the same as yersel'
I called for two gills of the best bitter beer
And she paid for them when they come in
And afore she'd swallied a half of hers
She says I would rather have gin
I caaled for a glass of the best Holland gin

And she swallied it doon the forst try
Says I to wor Nan, thoo's as good as a man
She says, Bob man, I feel very dry

Everybody joins in.

Chorus
And aye wor Nanny's a mazer
And a mazer she'll remain
As lang as I live I'll nivvor forget
The day we lost the train.

Matt *vamps.* **Barbara** *explains.*

Barbara   In the next stanza, this innocent woman, under
the influence of gin and an unfulfilled relationship with an
insensitive husband, decides to sing a song and attracts the
attention of the licensee. Her behaviour throughout is, of
course, a cry for help.

And they sing.

She sat and she drank till she got very tight
She says, Bob, I feel very queer
I says, tha's had nine glasses of gin
To my two gills of beer
She says, give us order I'll sing a bit song
I sat and glowered at her
I thowt she was jokin' for I'd nivvor heard
Wor Nanny sing any afore
She tried to get up for to sing 'The Cat Pie'
But she fell and she made such a clatter
She smashed fower chairs and the landlord come in
And he says, what the divil's the matter?

Everybody joins in.

Chorus
And aye wor Nanny's a mazer
And a mazer she'll remain
As lang as I live I'll nivvor forget
The day we lost the train.

Matt *vamps*. **Kate** *explains*.

Kate   In the final stanza, Bob and Nanny leave the pub
and go home. But the message cries to us across the
centuries. Never believe a story if a man's telling it.

And they sing.
He says to me, is this your wife?
And where do ye belang?
I says, it is and she's taken a fit
She's trying to sing a bit song
He wrung his arms around her waist
And trailed her ower the floor
And poor old Nan like a dorty hoos cat
Was hoyed outside the door
And there she was lyin' both groanin' and cryin'
To claim her I really felt shame
I tried to lift her and I couldn't shift her
I wished I'd had Nanny at yem
The paperman said he would give us a lift
So we hoisted her into the trap
But Nan was so tight that she couldn't sit up
So we fastened her down with a strap
She couldn't sit up and she wouldn't lie down
And she kicked till she shook the conveyance
She lost a new basket, a hat and a shawl
That woman with losin' her trains

And all join in for a Big Finish.

Chorus
And aye wor Nanny's a mazer
And a mazer she'll remain
As lang as I live I'll nivvor forget
The day we lost the train.

The song ends.

Darren *yells at them.*

Darren   Keep your positions! Don't move!

He waves at someone through the open door.

Reactions from the others: what the hell is the lad up to?

From outside there's the sound of a car, a sudden dazzle of headlights and a CRASH! as the front end of a Mini or such hits the doors of the club and stays there.

Darren (*yells*)   Thanks, lads!

A couple of kids get out of the car and run for it. We don't need to see them. Slamming doors will do.

He checks through his camera. Then he flings up his arm in triumph.

Yeah!

By this time the others have got their breath back.

Jacky   Hey! What you so excited about?

Darren   It's brilliant, man! I got the shot!

Jacky   Somebody just drove a car into the front door of the club. You're telling me that's brilliant?

Darren   Yes. It's all on camera.

Jacky *goes to the door.*

Fiona   A really interesting Tarantino shot, was it?

Darren   There wasn't any blood, like. But it's a start.

Then he calls to **Jacky** *who's at the door.*

What you doing?

Jacky   I'm looking for the little buggers that did this.

Darren   Don't waste your time. They'll be miles away by now.

Kate   So we can talk the whole thing over calmly and sensibly, can't we?

Darren   What is there to talk over?

Kate   You set that up, didn't you?

Darren   Set what up?

Kate   Oh, come on. This is your mother you're talking to.

Matt   Well, I couldn't help noticing you told us all not to move, and then you waved your hand, and the next thing there's a car crashing into the front door.

Darren   Well, yes, obviously, I set it up.

Barbara   But why?

Fiona   He wants to be Quentin Tarantino.

Barbara   You need a better reason than that.

Gazza   It's a good job he doesn't want to be Walt Disney. We'd all be elephants with big ears.

Barbara   And this isn't *Pulp Fiction*. This is a documentary. Isn't a documentary supposed to tell the truth?

Darren   This is the truth.

Matt   It isn't the truth if it's all rigged. It might be good enough for governments, but this is us we're talking about.

Darren   You and your traditions?

Matt   Spot on.

Darren   But they're all dead and gone. Same as this club. Admit it. The place is on its last legs.

He crosses to **Fiona**.

What did they tell you this afternoon? That this is the centre of the community?

Fiona   More or less. Though I suspect that's what I wanted to hear.

Darren   Either way it's a pack of lies. The club only opens at weekends and even then, nobody shows up. They can't raise a darts team. Nobody under thirty ever comes near the place.

Gazza   I do.

Darren   But you're a comedian.

Gazza   That's true. Well, partly true. I think.

Darren   And the next annual general meeting, they'll probably vote to close it down. Ask my dad. He's on the committee.

Fiona (*to* **Matt**)   Is that true?

Matt (*shuffly*)   Well, closure is one of a number of constructive possibilities we're looking into.

Darren   What other possibilities are there?

Matt   We'd thought of advertising for an eccentric millionaire.

Darren   It's very simple. We're talking about the death rattle of a traditional Tyneside working-men's club. That's the story. So you lot singing a daft old song while a couple of kids drive a stolen car through the front door, that says it all. I'm sorry. You want the truth. That's it. I wish it wasn't like that. But it is.

A silence, then:

Matt   Aye. The lad's right.

Jacky   Aye, I daresay.

Gazza   It's a pity but.

Barbara   A place where the men can sit and dream while the women go out to work.

Darren   Isn't that the story?

Kate   Of course it is.

Barbara   But it's cruel, for all that.

Kate   Cruel when you say it.

Barbara   Cruel to put it on television.

Jacky   There's no problem. They're not going to put it on television.

Darren   Oh, come on.

Fiona   Darren's the director.

Jacky   I mean, we've got choices here, haven't we?

Kate   Choices?

Barbara   That makes a change.

Jacky   On the one hand, there's direct action.

He crosses to the camera.

I could take this camera, remove the tape bearing the incriminating evidence, and hoy it in the river.

Darren   You can't do that.

Jacky   We could do it democratically. Take a vote. It's our traditions we're talking about. Democracy, that's part of the tradition. I can rig a vote with the best of them.

Gazza   Right then. I vote yes. I love chucking things in rivers, me. Big splashes. Great, man.

Jacky   Or there's peaceful persuasion.

Barbara   Oh. That old thing.

Jacky   I mean, everything the lad says is true. What we've got today is kids stealing cars, joyriding and ram-raiding and shoplifting and getting drunk and taking drugs. But that's not a tradition.

Barbara   Give it time.

Jacky   Traditions are leeks and working-men's clubs and the trade union movement . . .

Gazza   And whippets and folk songs . . .

Matt   And brass bands and lodge banners . . .

Barbara   And aunties and uncles with fanciful tales . . .

Darren And they've all gone.

Jacky But isn't that the point? We're talking about the past. We're talking about history.

Darren Ancient history.

Jacky And that's the only thing we've got any control over. We can't control the present or the future. But we can control the past. It's our ancient history. Nobody else's.

Barbara You want us to rewrite history?

Jacky Certainly I do. Isn't it the first thing all the bloody politicians do when they retire? Write their memoirs? Make sure they look good? I mean it wasn't *their* fault Tyneside's in such a mess, was it? Nothing's ever their fault.

Barbara Oh dear me, no. Never was. Never is.

Jacky So if *they're* entitled to rewrite history, so are we. We can rewrite it any way we choose. Because we carry it inside our heads. And I'll tell you this for nothing. We have no idea what's inside our heads till we start to look. It's like turning out an attic.

Gazza You're right there.

Matt You've been turning out your attic?

Gazza Don't be daft, man, I haven't got an attic, it's a maisonette.

Kate So what are you talking about?

Gazza The song. The folk song.

Barbara What about it?

Gazza I thought it was a mouldy old book I found in the reference library. And then, when we all started to sing, you know what? I knew it. I don't ever remember learning it, but I knew it. Is that what you're talking about?

Jacky That's what I'm talking about.

Fiona   What does the director think?

Darren   I think it's all very well but where are the pictures for the camera? All I can see is a manky bunch of leeks.

Jacky   Would you like to see the lodge banner?

Darren   The lodge banner?

Barbara   There isn't one.

Kate   It was never a proper lodge.

Jacky   There was never a Bedewell Colliery but . . .

He crosses to the door behind the bar.

Don't go away. Talk amongst yourselves. About your history.

And out he goes.

Barbara (*to the lads*)   Have you any idea what he's on about?

Matt   Not really.

Gazza   But that's nothing new. Half the time I don't know what anybody's on about.

Fiona   I think I know.

Kate   You do?

Fiona   Why aye.

Which naturally provokes a bit of a reaction, diverted as **Jacky** *returns carrying a rolled-up banner.*

Jacky   It's been locked away, by order of the committee, since Fiona's dad did his runner. Howay, give us a hand, man.

Matt *helps* **Jacky** *unfurl the banner. It's an exact replica of a genuine lodge banner. Across the top are the words BEDEWELL COLLIERY. Across the bottom are the words: WORKERS OF THE WORLD UNITE! There are three portraits on the banner.* **Fiona** *crosses to look more closely.*

Fiona   My father told me about this. He had it specially made.

Gazza   Who are the three fellers?

Barbara   Well, that's Karl Marx on the left, isn't it?

Fiona   Yes. That's Marx.

Jacky   And that one's Arthur Cook who led the General Strike in 1926.

Kate   Who's the other one? The face is familiar but . . .

Jacky   That's Tommy Carter.

Fiona   My dad.

Matt   It's a bit pushy, putting yourself between Karl Marx and Arthur Cook, isn't it?

Jacky   That's what the committee felt.

Fiona   He told me he once carried the banner in the miners' gala.

Jacky   He wanted to but he was told he wouldn't be made welcome, on account of being a fraud and an embezzler and a traitor to the working class.

Fiona   Yes. That sounds like Dad.

Barbara   It's a nice banner, mind. Barring the fact the feller in the middle's a criminal and there was never any such place as Bedewell Colliery.

Kate   Apart from that it's lovely.

Matt   Fifty per cent proof, I'd say.

Jacky   And do you suppose your television audience would know the difference between this and the real thing? Do you suppose they'd care? We're the only ones that know what's inside our heads. It's ours. Nobody else's. Without it, we're dead.

They stand back, admiring the banner. As they do so there's the sound of a police siren and a flashing blue light outside.

Barbara   Probably the fraud squad. Somebody been passing counterfeit lodge banners.

They look towards the door. In comes **Pat**. **Gazza**, *who crosses to her, gives her a hug and a kiss.*

Gazza   Hello, pet. What kept you?

Pat   The usual. Keeping the streets safe for pimps, hustlers and senior citizens.

She looks around.

What's going on here?

Gazza   We're making a documentary about our traditions and folk songs and leeks.

Pat   I see.

Gazza   This is Fiona, from the telly. Fiona, this is my wife, Pat.

Fiona   Yes. We met earlier.

Pat (*to* **Gazza**)   I popped in for a quick fix of Tamla Motown. (*Turns to* **Jacky**.) And I was proceeding in a westerly direction along your street and couldn't help but notice a car resting on your front door in a manner likely to cause an obstruction.

Darren   That's all part of the documentary.

Jacky   Something they tried but it didn't really work.

Matt   They probably won't use it.

Pat   So you don't want me to take any official action?

Jacky   There's no need.

Barbara   You could look for Fiona's wheels if you like.

Pat   You lost some wheels?

Fiona   From a Mercedes. Four.

Matt   Round ones.

Gazza   Never mind Fiona's wheels. Have you brought it?

Pat   Yes. It's in the car. Here.

She gives **Gazza** *the keys. He exits.* **Pat** *looks at the banner.*

The man in the middle? Tommy Carter?

Fiona   My dad. You know the face?

Pat   Professionally.

Fiona   What's he done now?

Pat   Something about time-share apartments in Spain. We had a fax from Interpol. Just routine, madam.

Fiona   It usually is.

Gazza *returns with a whippet on a lead.*

Gazza   See? They do exist!

Matt   Where did you get that?

Gazza   Belongs to my cousin Malcolm.

Pat   Uncle Bernard and Auntie Nancy. Their eldest.

Matt   That's a coincidence.

Jacky *starts organising* **Gazza**.

Jacky   If you and the dog stand there, in front of the banner. And we put the leeks on the table here.

He turns to **Fiona**.

I'm just working out the framing for the opening shot. Hey, it's a piece of piss being a director, isn't it? No wonder you people keep it to yourselves.

Darren   It's a travesty.

Fiona (*to* **Darren**)   Does the name John Ford mean anything to you?

Darren   You bet. My name's John Ford. I make westerns. *Stagecoach. She Wore a Yellow Ribbon. The Searchers.*

Fiona   He once said, given the choice between shooting the facts and shooting the legend, you should always shoot the legend.

Barbara   Shoot the legend. I like the sound of that.

Kate   Pity we don't have a band.

Gazza   Matty'll knock us out a bit tune.

Matt *puts his fingers to his lips.*

Matt   Listen . . .

Very quietly, magically, they hear the sound of a brass band.

Kate   Is that what I think it is?

Matt   I said it was a coincidence. Gazza's got a cousin Malcolm with a whippet. I've got a cousin Fred who plays in a band.

Kate   Uncle Davie and Auntie Winifred. Their youngest.

Matt   He wasn't sure how many he could manage at short notice but . . .

They listen. The music gets louder and louder. They're playing one of the great Geordie standards: for, preference, 'When the Boat Comes In'.

Jacky (*to* **Darren**)   Shall we shoot the legend, son?

Barbara   You know it makes sense.

Jacky   Look around you. It's the will of the people.

Darren *hesitates, then:*

Darren   Yes, bugger it! Let's shoot the legend!

He and **Fiona** *line up the camera.*

The others wait for the arrival of the band.

Fiona   'A Lovely Day for the Race'! Action!

Lights change.

The club walls disappear. Beyond them the great symbols of Tyneside: the bridges, shipyards and pitheads.

The band – as many as we can assemble at short notice – marches on.

Everybody joins in the chorus. A huge finish.

I can't follow that.

Wittgenstein on Tyne

Lee Hall

Wittgenstein on Tyne was originally performed at the Live Theatre, Newcastle-upon-Tyne, as part of a cycle of new plays presented in two parts entitled *Twelve Tales of Tyneside*, on 16 May 1997. The cast was as follows:

Ludwig Wittgenstein	Donald McBride
Mrs Britton	Charlie Hardwick
Sandra	Sharon Percy
Clark Cable	Joe Caffrey
Mr Braithwaite	Trevor Fox

Directed by Max Roberts
Designed by Perry John Hudson

Editor's Note

This is one of the funniest and rudest plays one could ever be asked to direct. Lee's professional debut as a playwright was made as part of a large-scale project entitled *Twelve Tales of Tyneside*. The production marked the reopening of the theatre on the quayside following extensive refurbishment and expansion. Under the editorial direction of Peter Flannery, who also wrote the prologue and one of the tales, Live commissioned twelve writers to create an epic cycle of plays that told a story of Tyneside, its past, present and future, at a time when so much of the region's rich industrial heritage was crumbling and finally succumbing to the new Thatcher order.

We discovered that Ludwig Wittgenstein had spent time during the Second World War as a hospital porter in the Newcastle General Hospital and the opportunity seemed to Lee too good to miss. It also allowed him to write for specific actors he had known and grown up with. Everything in the play is true.

Characters

Ludwig Wittgenstein, *a philosopher*
Mrs Britton, *his landlady*
Sandra, *her daughter*
Clark Cable (**Young Lad**), *a market gardener*
Mr Braithwaite, *a local air-raid warden*

Whistling in the dark. Beethoven.

A very tight spot snaps up on **Wittgenstein**'s *face. He is whistling.*

Wittgenstein   Ludwig Wittgenstein. Born Vienna, 1889.

He carries on whistling. He is enjoying himself.

The world's greatest living philosopher.

He carries on whistling.

Solved the major problems of philosophy. Twice. Professor of Philosophy, Cambridge University. Came to Newcastle, 1943. To work in the RVI. For the war effort. What is the use of sitting around thinking?

He whistles more Beethoven.

Prodigiously intelligent. Could whistle the whole of Beethoven. Very good, the whistling. Helps keep you relaxed, you know.

Continues whistling the Beethoven. Music swells under **Wittgenstein** *until it becomes loud and ecstatic. His head falls back as he is nearing orgasm and as the music reaches its climax an air-raid siren sounds. His face changes as the siren gets louder. He looks down anxiously at his crotch. We can't see anything except his face in the blackness.*

Suddenly a shaft of light illuminates him. He is receiving a blow job from a **Young Lad**. *A young girl,* **Sandra**, *comes running in. They both look anxiously at her and spring apart.* **Young Lad**'s *mouth is full and, not daring to swallow, he keeps his lips tightly closed.*

Mrs Britton, **Wittgenstein**'s *landlady, comes down the steps, following* **Sandra**.

Mrs Britton   Excuse me, Mr Wittgenstein, I hardly had time to put me teeth in.

Young Lad *still has his gob full and is looking the worse for wear.* **Sandra** *looks at the* **Young Lad** *suspiciously.*

Mrs Britton   I see you've got a nice young friend here.

Young Lad *still won't swallow.* **Sandra** *hands him a handkerchief. He spits in it discreetly, then wipes his mouth with his hand.*

Mrs Britton   Well, aren't you going to introduce us then?

Wittgenstein   This is Mr . . . Mr . . . ?

Young Lad   C-C-C-Cable.

He holds out his hand, then thoughtfully wipes it on his jacket.

C-C-Clark Cable.

Mrs Britton   Very pleased to meet you.

Sandra   Are you from the hospital too?

Young Lad   N-n-no, I just m-met Mr Witkinsteen and I was gi-giving him a b-b-b- –

Wittgenstein *looks in horror.*

Young Lad   B-bit of advice.

Mrs Britton   Advice?

Young Lad   About his marrow.

Sandra   But Mr Wittgenstein hasn't got any marrows.

Mrs Britton   He hasn't even got an allotment.

Wittgenstein   We were discussing the matter theoretically. (*To* **Young Lad**.) Yes, very interesting. I expect you have to be going.

Mrs Britton   But there's an air raid, Mr Wittgenstein.

Wittgenstein   It's all right, the lad has got his bike and he only lives in Elswick.

Sandra   You can't go out now, you might be killed.

Mrs Britton   You're more than welcome here, son.

Wittgenstein   But . . .

Mrs Britton   Mr Wittgenstein.

She looks down at **Wittgenstein**'s *crotch. He stares at her.*

You have egg on your chin.

Wittgenstein   I beg your pardon.

Mrs Britton   You have egg on your chin.

Wittgenstein *checks his chin.* **Mrs Britton** *stares at his flies to indicate subtly where the problem lies, but this simply encourages everyone to stare at* **Wittgenstein**'s *flies – which are undone.*

Sandra   Your flies are undone.

Wittgenstein *realises and quickly rectifies the matter.*

Mrs Britton   Mr Wittgenstein, it's not like you. You're usually very fastidious. Now, Mr Cable. How long have you known Mr Wittgenstein?

An explosion. The door bursts open. In comes **Mr Braithwaite**.

Braithwaite   They've hit Peggy Rodger's. The place is a right state.

Sandra   Hello, Mr Braithwaite.

Braithwaite   Hello, Sandra.

Mrs Britton   This is Mr Wittgenstein, our lodger, and his nice young friend, Mr Cable. He's a market gardener or something.

Braithwaite   I beg your pardon?

Mrs Britton   A market gardener.

Braithwaite   Don't I know you?

Young Lad   I d-d-don't think so.

Braithwaite   You're the little bastard in the Dog and Parrot.

Mrs Britton   The Dog and Parrot?

Sandra   It's a queer bar.

Mrs Britton   What were you doing in an unusual bar, Mr Braithwaite? I understood you were teetotal.

Braithwaite   I was caught a bit short when I was passing through town. I stopped at the aforementioned hostelry not realising its provenance, and as I was relieving myself I was accosted by this gentleman.

Mrs Britton   Mr Cable! You attacked Mr Braithwaite? He fought in the Somme, you know.

Young Lad   I never attacked nobody.

Mrs Britton   What exactly did he do to you, Mr Braithwaite?

Braithwaite   He made improper suggestions.

Mrs Britton   I'm not sure I understand.

Sandra   Mam.

Mrs Britton   Where is this place exactly?

Sandra   Down the end of Pilgrim Street.

Braithwaite   So, Mr Cable. What the hell are you doing in here?

Mrs Britton   Mr Cable came with Mr Wittgenstein. To talk about leeks.

Braithwaite   I don't believe you know the first thing about horticulture. Do you, lad?

He grabs **Young Lad**.

When would you normally pot a geranium? Eh?

Young Lad *looks blank.*

Braithwaite   You don't know, do you?

Young Lad   N-n-no.

Braithwaite   Exactly.

Sudden silence.

Mrs Britton   So what exactly were you both doing down here, Mr Wittgenstein?

Sandra   Mam.

Mrs Britton   Don't you Mam me.

Sandra   It's obvious.

Mrs Britton   What's obvious?

Sandra   He wanted a blow job.

Mrs Britton   Mr Wittgenstein, is it true you brought this young man down here to give him a job?

Sandra   Mam. Mr Cable was giving it to Mr Wittgenstein.

Mrs Britton   But Mr Wittgenstein is gainfully employed.

Sandra   A blow job isn't a job, Mam.

Mrs Britton   Well, what the hell is it?

Sandra   It means getting your knob sucked.

Mrs Britton   Where on earth did you hear of such a thing?

Sandra   Mr Braithwaite told me.

Mrs Britton   Mr Braithwaite, is this true?

Braithwaite   I may have mentioned it in passing.

Mrs Britton   I've never heard anything like this. Let me get this right. Mr Wittgenstein brought nice young Mr Cable down here for a sexual purpose?

Sandra   Yes.

Mrs Britton   Well, who were they going to have sex with?

Braithwaite   With each other.

Mrs Britton   But you're both men.

Braithwaite   They're a couple of turd burglars.

Wittgenstein   Sir, I resent your tone.

Braithwaite   Christ. Not a Kraut 'n' all.

Wittgenstein   I am not a Kraut.

Braithwaite   That's exactly what you are. A bleeding wurst swallower.

Wittgenstein   I am an Austrian. It was I who was annexed.

Mrs Britton   We'll have less of that sort of language, Mr Wittgenstein. I can't quite believe what I'm hearing. You brought poor Mr Cable down here simply to do this horrible act. Isn't it unhygienic?

Braithwaite   Poor Mr Cable! He was trying to do the same to me in the bloody Dog and Parrot.

Mrs Britton   You as well, Mr Braithwaite. What on earth is the world coming to?

Braithwaite   Let me assure you, madam, I declined the young gentleman's proposition in no uncertain terms.

Mrs Britton   But Mr Wittgenstein, I don't understand. You always pay your rent on time.

Braithwaite   It's disgusting.

Sandra   Actually, I think it's quite romantic.

Mrs Britton   Romantic.

Braithwaite   Quite romantic. It was hard-nosed buggery. There's our lads laying down their lives for King and country and you two are down here messing about like a pair of Greek bosuns.

Young Lad   Don't call me a b-bosun.

Braithwaite   I'll call you what I like. You Kraut gobbler.

Wittgenstein   Will you stop inferring I am German?

Braithwaite   Well, what are you then?

Mrs Britton   He's a hospital porter.

Wittgenstein   I am not a hospital porter.

Mrs Britton   Yes you are.

Wittgenstein   I am a technician.

Mrs Britton   Well, that's news to me.

Braithwaite   You don't look like a technician.

Mrs Britton   Mr Braithwaite's a technician, aren't you?

Sandra   And he has a club foot.

Mrs Britton   Sandra, please.

Wittgenstein   I *am* a technician. In the hospital.

Braithwaite   I bet you're not trained, though.

Wittgenstein   No, I am not a trained technician. I am a trained philosopher.

Amazed silence.

Braithwaite   A philosopher?

Wittgenstein   Indeed.

Young Lad   You n-never told me you were a philosopher.

Wittgenstein   You never asked.

Braithwaite   You're taking the piss.

Mrs Britton   Language.

Wittgenstein   On the contrary. I am indeed a trained philosopher.

Braithwaite (*sarcastically*)   I bet that's kept you in work.

Wittgenstein   Sir, I held a chair in Cambridge.

Braithwaite Exactly.

Sandra He means he was Professor of Philosophy.

Mrs Britton At Cambridge.

Braithwaite A right clever shite.

Wittgenstein Sir, I have an international reputation.

Mrs Britton So what exactly is this philosophy of yours, Mr Wittgenstein?

Braithwaite To go round shagging young boys in foreign countries?

Wittgenstein No, sir, my philosophy is of a technical nature, questioning traditional notions of metaphysics as related to the epistemology of language.

Braithwaite How many people believe in your philosophy, Mr Clever Clogs.

Wittgenstein About two?

Sandra Two?

Young Lad It can't be much c-cop then.

Braithwaite You be quiet.

Wittgenstein Just because it is not fully understood does not make it erroneous. The ignorance of one man does not detract from the wisdom of another. Logic, I'm afraid, is undemocratic.

Braithwaite Can you understand a word he's saying?

Sandra He's saying, even if notions of truth and value are relative, the logical processes inherent in the language with which we make these judgements are absolute.

Mrs Britton I've warned you, Sandra.

Braithwaite Well, if you're so bloody clever, how come you're a hospital porter, eh?

Wittgenstein   I am not a hospital porter.

Braithwaite   Well, what the hell are you doing in Newcastle? Why aren't you off philosophising somewhere?

Wittgenstein   What is the point of philosophy in wartime? Surely you'd rather I worked shoulder to shoulder with people dignified by practical labour than sanctimoniously sitting round pontificating.

Braithwaite   What do you think you're doing now?

Wittgenstein   But I need to be with ordinary people. Not arid academics.

Mrs Britton   People like us?

Wittgenstein   Yes.

Braithwaite   Don't call me ordinary, pal, I've fought in the Somme.

Young Lad   I h-h-hope you're not t-t-trying to patronise us.

Wittgenstein   I'm not trying to patronise anybody.

Braithwaite   Who do you think you are? Coming over here, spouting philosophy and bumming our gardeners?

Wittgenstein   I don't think I'm anybody. Just because I am a philosopher, or a professor, or an aristocrat or an Austrian doesn't mean I'm any more important than any of you.

Young Lad   Aristocrat. You're telling me I've been s-s-shagging an aristocrat. Me dad'll kill us.

Mrs Britton   Surely not a socialist *and* an invert.

Wittgenstein   But that is the point. Just because I come from an aristocratic background doesn't mean I am an aristocrat.

Braithwaite   I don't know how else you become one.

Wittgenstein   But I have given my entire fortune away. All I own is a deckchair and the complete works of Tolstoy. What does that make me? I am no longer an aristocrat. I am a philosopher.

Braithwaite   Philosopher my arse. Listen, mate, you're a flipping bum bandit.

Wittgenstein   But what does it mean to say I am nothing but this bum bandage? What do you mean?

Braithwaite   Exactly what I said. A shirtlifter.

Wittgenstein   But, sir, what do you mean by 'meaning'?

Braithwaite   What do you mean, what do I mean by meaning?

Wittgenstein   Precisely that. What is the meaning of meaning?

Braithwaite   Well, meaning is the meaning.

Wittgenstein   If 'meaning is the meaning' you have said precisely nothing at all. A logical tautology.

Mrs Britton   Hang on a minute.

Wittgenstein   OK, a simple example. What, for instance, does 'five' mean?

Braithwaite   Er. It's five things.

Wittgenstein   Five things are five things. I put it to you again what is 'five', sir?

Braithwaite   Five is five.

Wittgenstein   But what does it mean? Define it.

Braithwaite *is blank.*

Sandra   It's between 'four' and 'six'.

Wittgenstein   Excellent. Five derives its meaning through being between 'four' and 'six'. But what is four and six?

Mrs Britton   Not much these days.

Wittgenstein   Four is after three and before five. And et cetera ad infinitum. Do you see?

Braithwaite   You've lost me, pal.

Wittgenstein   What is a table?

Young Lad   S-something to put things on.

Wittgenstein   But if I sit on it? Is it a chair? A table is a table because it isn't a chair. It only has 'meaning' because we can put it in its place in our linguistic system.

Sandra   So it's just a way of describing things. There is no real 'meaning'.

Young Lad   Eh?

Sandra   Like in a dictionary. If you look up one word to find out what it means, it only gives you another word. So you look up those words and they only refer you to other words and so you go round in circles.

Wittgenstein   Precisely. You see, there is no 'meaning', only a linguistic description. A language game. There is no essence. I ask you what is an Austrian? You say not an American. Not a German. This is good. But then I ask you what *is* an Austrian. And you say . . . ?

Young Lad   S-s-someone from Austria.

Wittgenstein   But what *is* this person?

Braithwaite   A bloody arsehole.

Mrs Britton   Mr Braithwaite!

Wittgenstein   What is this person? A Jew? A communist? A speaker of German? A homosexual? Who exactly are you talking about? What exactly does this person mean? You cannot define a person. A person does not mean anything. The whole idea of 'meaning' is totally redundant.

Braithwaite   I don't know what this has got to do with anything.

Sandra   I do.

Mrs Britton   Shut up, Sandra.

Sandra   It's got to do with everything.

Wittgenstein   You are desperate to give things a meaning. Some reductive fixed meaning, so you can define them. And once you can define them, you can control them. And once you can control them, you can only put them in boxes and bury them in the ground. But the only way to do this is to fix a meaning where logically there isn't one. What is a book? It just is. What is the sun? It just is. What is God? What is life? What is you? What is I? It just is. Sir, I am a German speaker. I am a Jew. I am a poof. But let me tell you all is not what it seems. I am not a German or a Jew or a poof. I am only me.

Mrs Britton   Could you run through that again?

Braithwaite   You come over here dipping your wick and now you're lecturing us with your highfalutin' ideas about the meaninglessness of the meaning of meaning. I should kick your arse right back to Baden-Munich.

Sandra   There's nothing wrong with his ideas.

Braithwaite   Nothing wrong with his ideas!?

Sandra   I quite like them.

Mrs Britton   Sandra, love, it's people with ideas that have got us to the mess we're in today.

Braithwaite   It's all right for you rich bastards, but I've never had the opportunity to sit around thinking.

Sandra   What about when you're on the allotment?

Braithwaite   I'm too busy gardening.

Sandra   Even in the potting shed?

Mrs Britton   But, Mr Wittgenstein, if there isn't any meaning, this is terrible.

Braithwaite   What about God?

Wittgenstein   Recognising the limits of our own patterns of thinking is the only way to truly contemplate the unknown and the unknowable. Philosophy is the truest form of spiritual contemplation. But it is not about answers, it is about questions. Questioning our very prejudice.

Young Lad   If there isn't any answers, what about s-s-science, then? There's plenty of answers in science.

Wittgenstein   Science has no answers. What is the answer to life? The only answer science can give is 'death'. Yesterday I walked past a bookshop. In one window were the books of Freud and Einstein; in the other pictures of Schubert and Beethoven. And I saw where we have come in one hundred years. Is the universe any more profound because of Mr Einstein? Are our minds any more fathomable because of Mr Freud? All these sciences: linguistics, economics, sociologies. They ask how big, how small, how many. We all become numbers. And when we are numbers we can be erased. This is science. But listen to Beethoven and there are no answers. There are no simple equations. Mr Beethoven is asking what makes us human. What we have lost is a world not where there are endless answers and solutions, but where there are mysteries. This is what I have learnt. The first lesson of all philosophy is inimical to science. It is that we know nothing. Philosophy is a religion of disbelief. All about us is a mystery we cannot begin to encompass, thus the only logical thing to do is to ask what is human about ourselves. We have reached the stage that it is easier to destroy the whole world than to discover oneself. And this is science. This is the so-called answer. Even as we speak they are making bombs to blow up entire cities and we sit and argue about where I put my penis. I wonder what we have become. I wonder what we have become.

Mrs Britton I think you are over-analysing things, Mr Wittgenstein.

Sandra How can you over-analyse something?

Mrs Britton When you haven't got time for anything else.

Braithwaite It seems he's got plenty of time to go buggering about in air-raid shelters.

Wittgenstein People are dropping bombs on us.

Braithwaite But it just isn't British.

Wittgenstein Then you must be unfamiliar with the English public school system.

Braithwaite Don't start being smart with me. At least I'm not a Kraut.

Wittgenstein What is this 'British' with its brambly hedgerows and warm beers and pillar boxes and Oxo cubes and pound cakes and dog-eared parsons and village greens and interminable Sundays. It is a nation of mindless sentimentality. Passionless prejudice, terrified of sex, of idea, of strangers, of living. This is the only modern European nation that has not had a revolution, not because there is no poverty, inequality or injustice, but because of your sure bloody complacency. You let your bosses keep you ignorant and your peers make you feel proud of it. Thinking has nothing to do with poverty. A poor man can think just as clearly as a rich man. Sainthood has always been predicated on it. No, you make yourselves poor because your lives are unexamined. Because all your nostalgia has made you sick. And that's why I hate your Blitz spirit, your happy-go-lucky working-class humour, and your shepherd's pies, and your sooty terraces, and knockabouts of a Sunday. Because it is an unthinking excuse for your lack of real endeavour. This is what I hate in Britain. And this is why I hate every last one of you cheeky cheery Geordie fools.

Young Lad L-listen, I just gave you a blow job.

Sandra   I'm not complacent.

Braithwaite   That's it. I've had enough.

He takes his stick.

What will it mean if I smash your ruddy heads together?

Wittgenstein   It won't mean anything. You club-footed cretin.

Braithwaite *takes a swing at* **Wittgenstein**. *He misses but clunks* **Young Lad** *on the head. He is felled.*

Mrs Britton   Stop it at once.

Sandra (*trying to stop* **Mr Braithwaite**'s *assault*)   You never complained when I gave *you* a blow job.

Everybody stops.

Mrs Britton   You did what?

Sandra   He said it was a lollipop.

Young Lad   See, you h-hypocritical bastard.

He dies.

Mrs Britton (*reprimanding* **Young Lad**)   Hey! (*To* **Sandra**.) I don't believe this.

Sandra   I got his coupons.

Mrs Britton   But, Sandra, you're only thirteen.

Sandra   But, Mam, after all, he fought in the Somme.

Young Lad   How c-c-come he fought in the Somme if he had a club foot, eh?

He dies again.

Everyone looks at **Braithwaite**.

Braithwaite   I never actually said I 'fought' in the Somme.

Mrs Britton   I bet you never left Shieldfield.

Mrs Britton *takes a swipe at* **Braithwaite** *with a kettle. She kills him.*

Sandra   I think you've killed Mr Braithwaite, Mam.

Mrs Britton *falls to the ground in grief.* **Wittgenstein** *stares at the carnage around him.*

Wittgenstein   Let's try and be philosophical about this.

Sandra   What's that meant to mean?

Wittgenstein   I'm fucked if I know. This is what I am trying to tell you.

The sound of all clear.

Sandra   That's the all-clear.

Wittgenstein   All-clear?

The faint sound of a doodlebug. Getting louder.

Wittgenstein   Well, I guess I'll see you at breakfast.

The sound of a huge explosion. White light blinds the audience.

Music: Beethoven.

Blackout.

Laughter When We're Dead

Sean O'Brien

What's the matter, you dissentious rogues,
That rubbing the poor itch of our opinion,
Make yourselves scabs?

Coriolanus

Laughter When We're Dead was first performed at the Live Theatre, Newcastle-upon-Tyne, on 14 June 2000, with the following cast:

William Farr	Dave Whitaker
James Jackson MP	Deka Walmsley
Elizabeth Jackson	Libby Davison
Richard Tallow	Michael Hodgson
Gregor Glass	Donald McBride
Daisy Gates	Suzy Cooper
Football Supporter	Rob Atkinson
Denise	Grace Stilgrove
Gadgee	Dave Whitaker
Bobby Brammer	Michael Hodgson
Miranda	Sasha Pick
Eddie Robson	Donald McBride
Woman at club	Libby Davison
Commentator 1	Mike Neville
Commentator 2	Laura Lindow

Directed by Max Roberts
Designed by Perry John Hudson

Editor's Note

A remarkable dramatic debut from Sean O'Brien, who
responded to a brief to write a verse drama for Live with a
political theme. He produced the following classically
constructed revenge tragedy in five acts, in rhyming
pentameters, about a Tyneside-born local MP and Home
Secretary attending a 'future' Labour Party Conference at
Whitley Bay. It contains some phenomenal writing.

Characters

William Farr, *poet*
James Jackson, *Home Secretary*
Elizabeth Jackson, *lawyer, married to Jackson*
Richard Tallow, *Prime Minister*
Gregor Glass, *Tallow's adviser*
Daisy Gates, *Jackson's Private Parliamentary Secretary*
Football Supporter
Denise, *barmaid/waitress*
Gadgee
Bobby Brammer, *Jackson's Party agent*
Miranda, *daughter of Elizabeth and Jackson*
Eddie Robson, *councillor*
Woman
Heavy
Commentator 1
Commentator 2

Staging

In the production at Live Theatre, Newcastle, the acting space was organised as follows. Downstage left represented the living room and the exteriors such as the working-men's club and the bridge pillars/riverside. Upstage, elevated, was the office/domestic area. Stage right was the bar/podium. Centre stage was the hotel room, with the settee which was also, on occasion, the settee in the bar area.

Prologue

1984.

Lights up on old wooden-armed settee, TV, room heated by Calor gas heater. **Farr**, *sprawled on settee half under a blanket in T-shirt and underpants, is watching the news on television. Sounds of public disturbance are faintly audible from it. He's drinking a can of beer with a whisky chaser. Books and typing paper are scattered at his feet.*

Farr (*trying out a couplet on himself*)
'The omelette of the revolution begs
The question: what to tell the eggs.'
Oh, dear, oh dear. What total bloody shite.
William, you're just too – pissing – pissed to write.
'In the destructive element immerse' –
Bad for your liver; lethal for your verse.

Enter **James Jackson**. *He carries a bucket (apparently full of small change), decorated with NUM stickers, and a megaphone, similarly decorated.*

The talk between **Farr** *and* **Jackson** *is aggressively friendly, heavily sarcastic, and ironical in the way of young men.* **Farr** *is not as confident or insouciant as he cares to suggest.* **Jackson**, *on the other hand, is quite certain of himself even in the context of imminent political defeat. They are close friends who no longer know what they think about each other.*

Farr (*toasts* **Jackson** *ironically*)
Young James. I saw you on the box just then,
The ugly one stood next to Tony Benn.

Jackson *puts down bucket and sits on arm of settee. Both gaze at the television.*

Jackson
Really, William? Where the hell were you?

Farr
The Muse had other work for me to do.
As you can see, I've laboured here since dawn

To get the people's new creation born.
What revolution really needs is art.

Jackson (*takes a can*)
Away and shite. Budge up, you drunken fart.

Sits on arm of settee.

What's Thatcher said about us all today?

Farr
The usual. We're in the Kremlin's pay,
And those of us who aren't are idle dupes
Who'll get what for when she sends in the troops.
Of course, she didn't actually say that,
But she does find the gathered proletariat
A menace to the fabric of the West . . .
Hang on a sec. I like this next bit best –
They've shown it . . . must be seven times now, right?
– Here comes the tooled-up army of the night.
The coppers, like the Tsarist cavalry,
Ride down the pickets. See now. There's this tree –

Acts out what he describes.

And some lad's pulled himself right up the trunk –
He's swaying in the wind, he's mortal drunk –
And what's he got? – a fuckin megaphone,
As if he might succeed with 'words alone'
In turning back McGregor's coal-black tide.

Turns the TV off. Sits down again. Pause.

D'you ever think we've backed the losing side?

Jackson
The day we hang the scabs from every light
Along the quays you won't say that.

Shakes his head.

                                          You're right.
We've lost this one. We lost it from the start.
We just can't stand to say we're losing heart.

Unless the bloody movement gets behind
The struggle – and it won't – well, then we'll find
By Christmas that the numbers haemorrhage.
Come April we'll be on the inside page.
The Labour Party's sold its birthright now:
You've got to hand it to that Thatcher cow.

Jackson *drinks deeply from can.*

Farr
I only asked.

Jackson
                  Give us another beer.
So this –

Picks up sheaf of paper and looks through it, discarding sheets as he goes.
                  is what you've been achieving here.
Haikus, limericks, doodles, clerihews –
But sweet fuck all that anyone can use.
A poet can't just sit around and booze.

Farr
Well then, get me opium or speed.
To each, you know, 'according to his need'.
I can't help it if I've got the block.

Jackson
And therefore you lie in and scratch your cock,
Take public money for a PhD
You'll never finish, stare at the TV
And like to think

Gestures at room.

                  that this is politics.
All poets, Comrade Farr, are useless pricks.

Snatches away blanket.

Farr (*snatching it back*)
And Party hacks are policemen in disguise.
But Jacksy, since you mention pricks, then why's

The beautiful Elizabeth not here?
I hoped she might come bearing extra beer,
A servant of the great god Dionysos,
The kind of girl you need when there's a crisis.

Jackson
She'll be here soon. She had someone to meet.

Farr
I'd love to be the dark end of her street.
A girl like that, a radiant English rose,
You'd think she'd go for poetry, not prose.
I can't imagine what she sees in you.

Jackson
No, William, I don't suppose you do.

Farr
What's mine is yours. That's always been the case.

Jackson
You touch her and I'll melt your fucking face.

Farr
I'm going, Jacksy, honest. Look, I've gone.

Jackson
Right. Don't forget to put your trousers on.

Exit **Farr**.

Jackson *turns the television back on.*

Enter **Elizabeth**. **Jackson** *does not hear her come in and is gripped by events on screen. She stands watching him.*

TV Current Affairs Commentator
Nationwide, the police on double time
Are bussed in hundreds to the picket line –

Jackson
Indulging an insensitive display
Of V-signs to the miners in their way
Or pressing fivers to the steamy glass

To taunt the opposition as they pass.
The pitmen, though they're fighting for their lives,
Reply that they've been shagging coppers' wives –

Commentator
Meanwhile the sequestrators' long pursuit
Of union funds looks to be bearing fruit.
From Paris via Alpine Liechtenstein
Officials followed Scargill's credit line–

Jackson *gets up and turns the sound down on the television. Now he notices* **Elizabeth**.

Jackson
Elizabeth. Look, I was miles away.

Elizabeth
I know that, James. It's what you always say.
When James is talking to you, you can see
That his attention's fixed on history,
The bigger picture on the TV screen –
What ought to be, or else what might have been.
In triumph Lenin crosses the Tyne Bridge.
Meanwhile I bet there's nothing in the fridge
But lager for that pisshead William Farr –

Jackson
Why don't you simply tell me how you are?

Elizabeth
I've done it, James. The child, it's gone. That's it.
I've done it, James. It didn't hurt a bit.

Pause.

So you stay here and watch your bridges burn
And meanwhile I'll have something in return.
I'm taking up the scholarship. The flight's
From London. I'll go down tomorrow night.

Jackson
Well, then.

Elizabeth
> Well, then. Look, I've got things to do.
You're obviously busy.

Jackson
> > I love you.

Elizabeth
Yes.

Jackson
> I mean it.

Elizabeth
> > Yes, you've said.

Jackson
> > > Give me a call?

Elizabeth
Yes. Anyway. It's gone. That's really all.

Jackson
Lizzy –

Elizabeth
> It's just a year. So then let's see
What's what. All right?

Looks at TV.

> > There's Scargill on TV.

Jackson's *gaze is drawn inevitably to the screen.* **Elizabeth** *waits
a few seconds, then exits. After a pause,* **Jackson** *looks round to see
her gone. He stares after her for a little while, then turns the sound up
on the TV: the Orgreave riot, cries, panic, a horseback baton charge,
growing louder. Blackout.*

Act One

Scene One

The near future.

TV announcer's voice is heard. **James Jackson** *MP, Home Secretary, watching TV from large leather settee in hotel room while preparing to go out, tying shoelaces, putting on tie, etc.*

Announcer
Addressing the Party conference today,
Staged this year in refurbished Whitley Bay –
A move seen as a nod towards tradition –
The PM boldly stated his position.
Departing eloquently from his text,
Richard Tallow laid out what the next
New Labour government would have in mind
For Britain, even though they're far behind
Portillo's Tories in the latest polls.
The PM spoke of struggling for the souls
Of the excluded and the rich alike.
Equipped with nothing but a mike
He gripped the hall with passion and commitment –

Jackson *switches sound off on remote.*

Jackson
– So no one really wondered what this shit meant.
After ideology comes noise –
So, on the count of three, then, girls and boys.

Lights up upstage right. **Richard Tallow**, *Prime Minister, is speaking at podium. Behind him is a banner carrying the slogan 'Labour Speaks for England'.* **Tallow** *and the banner are also projected on to a large screen at one side of the stage.*

Intermittent vast applause. Also present to one side, seated in the 'office' area, is **Gregor Glass**, *who mouths the words of the speech silently, checking them against his written text, occasionally shaking his head with disapproval at the delivery, or nodding with satisfaction that*

his intention has been conveyed. At some points we hear **Glass**
speaking the words, though **Tallow** *is still mouthing them and
performing his repertoire of appealingly 'inclusive' gestures.*

Tallow
Never before has such opportunity
Offered itself to the people of Britain.
Never before such a chance within reach
To free the power of enterprise, the power
I like to call imagination, and to smash
The past's taboos, its strife and sentiment,
I say, I mean, I really do, I say –

Glass *looks skyward.*

Tallow
To smash all that, to earn our way towards
That New Jerusalem our founders surely meant –
The true just city on the high green hill –
The true just city on the high green hill
The England which our kids will live to see.
I like to call it England, PLC.

Applause.

And this is why we cannot tolerate,
No, this is why we *dare* not tolerate,
No, this is why we *must* not tolerate
Those who will not contribute, who stand apart,
Or rather sit apart, who live apart

Glass
In lager-stinking dens, the TV on
By day to watch the shopping channel, and by night
To bathe in porn. My friends, I ask,

Tallow
                              my friends,
These people are not *England*, are they? No!
Are we these people, England, England? No!

Vast 'No!' from the audience.

These people are the past, the easy life,

Glass
Do-nothing, pass the lager, I'm all right,

Tallow
The fatty tissue England now can ill afford.
The long-term unemployed, I hear you say,
The unemployable. *Who's* unemployable?

Applause.
No one I know. No one you know either.
My wife's grandad sadly lost a leg –
He had an accident while down the pit
(Now that was *work*.) And did he skive
And whinge?

Glass
                        And did he watch TV? Oh, no.

Tallow
This was the Depression. This was Means Test.
This was workhouse waiting down the road.
Grandad, to coin a phrase, got on his bike.
Today, of course, some idler in the street
Would steal my grandad's bike to sell –

Applause.

Lights back up on **Jackson** *watching the rerun on TV in hotel room.*

Jackson
At which point I would have to intervene
And chop his fucking hand off. Oh, you can't deny
We're hard as fuck on evil nowadays –
Since that's the only policy that plays
Down where the Morlocks 'read' the *Daily Mail* –
Let's put the lot where they belong, in jail –
Graffiti artists, bike thieves, teenage mums,
We make 'em stand up straight and do their sums,
And those who stain the fabric of the State
Will find they've left repentance much too late –

All guaranteed to madden liberal whingers.
Next up we're burning gyppos. As for gingers . . .
Watch it. Oh we're hard because we're hard
Because by being hard we're being kind.
Because one day a world ago
The Leader read a book and lost his mind.

Pause.

Once your direction's been decided, then
The task is just to organise the men –
Was that said by Lenin, or by Beria,
Or Trotsky? Somewhere in that area.
Anyway, you get my general drift:
The management of every rightward shift
Anticipates where possible, then smothers
Uproar from the tankies; fuck off, brothers.

Pause.

There's one thing I learned way back from the Reds:
There's bosses, right. There's Party. Then there's Neds.
They turn out when requested, make their mark,
Or stay at home to populate the dark,
The shadow cast by realpolitik
Which lengthens, darkens, even as we speak.
It's not enough to keep the South on board:
The North's a luxury we can't afford –
Except for us they've nowhere left to be:
They're ours, and we've thrown away the key:
What people need is someone else to hate:
Scapegoats, courtesy of Nanny State –
Asylum seekers, gypsies, paedophiles,
Whoever takes their minds off death and piles.
This year the Conference came to Whitley Bay,
To make these arseholes think they've had their say –
Union knackers, councillors in clover–
Stand up, shut your mouths and now bend over.
My wife complains I've lost the power to feel.
But I was made by this machine: that's real.
A rude mechanical, I'll make it mine,
And in its works I'll prosper or decline . . .

Le'etat c'est moi, so Tallow says,
But Middle England's counting down the days
And now young Jacksy's going out to play.
Is Jacks a dull boy? Is he fuck! No way!

Jackson *calls* **Daisy Gates** *on the mobile. Lights up on* **Daisy**
on upstage 'office' area. She is partially dressed, in a skirt and slip.

Jackson
What are you wearing?

Daisy
                          What am I wearing?
Why d'you want to know?

Jackson
                              Because it makes me hard
To think you're in that fishnet leotard.

Daisy
That's a good guess, Jacksy, but you're wrong.

Jackson
Suspenders and black stockings and a thong?

Daisy
You're just a sweet old-fashioned sort of bloke.

Jackson
I think adultery should be baroque.

Daisy
Well, Uncle, you'll just have to wait and see,
Or come round now to watch me while I pee.

Jackson
Later. I've got tickets for the match –
But then I'll drink ambrosia from your snatch.
I take it you'll be lunching with the boss.

Daisy
And so should you. You'll only make him cross.
And Glass considers it's 'appropriate'
That you and Tallow use this lunch to state
That talk of your estrangement's misconceived –

Jackson (*amused*)
Although it's Glass who gets these tales believed?
It's terrible. My loyalties are split.
The Toon or Richard Tallow? Fuck that shit.
Daisy woman man, I live in fear.
Just keep an eye on Gregor Glass, you hear?
See all, say nowt, then whisper in my bed
The things they meant as well as what they said.

Blackout on **Jackson**. *As she speaks,* **Daisy** *puts on a blouse and jacket, inspecting herself in the mirror of the audience.*

Daisy
Oh, Daisy, Daisy Gates, you do have fun.
The first time I went down, the time we won,
I sat with all the other girls and smiled,
Coiffured and buffed and corporately styled
In rosy suits, the ladies of the law.
They'd won their seats and thought they'd won the war.
They showed a leg to please the fourth estate
(Who from now on will always lie in wait)
That day outside the palace on the green,
Then disappeared as if they'd never been.
Designed, you will remember, by a bloke,
Westminster simply swallowed them like smoke.
The first time I went down, I knew the score:
Don't be the kind of girl the boys ignore
Until they need you on to read the script:
You might as well be living in a crypt.
The person and the project are the thing:
Don't wait for the division bell to ring.
Much wiser to become a PPS:
I've found my talent lies in saying yes
To rooms like this and randy afternoons
On corridors patrolled by wired goons
With guns and inside legs like Sly Stallone.
Much nicer this way than to be alone.
Of course, I'm not a feminist as such:
They look like dykes. They think too bloody much.

Scene Two

Dusk.

Enter a football **Crowd**, *black-and-white shirts and scarves, chanting, clapping, breath rising in clouds.* **Jackson** *enters with them and sits on the back of the settee, with his feet on the cushions.*

Crowd
Peter Reid, Peter Reid,
Peter Reid's got a monkey's heid.

Crowd *gasps at a near miss, then roars in disapproval.*

Crowd
The referee's a cunt, the referee's a cunt.
He's got his fookin arse on back to fookin front.

A goal is scored. Uproar.

A **Supporter** *makes himself noticed gesturing passionately at (we guess) the referee.*

Supporter
Shoveitupyerfuckinarseyeradgiefuckintwat!

The other supporters stare at him in disapproval for speaking 'solo'.

Hey, I'd bet he's *nae* idea who the fuck said that!

Jackson
There is a spectre haunting Europe, right?
So watch out Real Madrid next Wednesday night –
For when the Toon gets in among you; then
We'll see who's only lasses and who's men –
Although the crowd's inhuman single voice
Is all, I find, that still lets me rejoice.

Supporter
Refe*ree*!
Yer couldn't find your arse with both hands and a light –
Yer fuckin bag of fuckin Mackem shite!

Jackson
These are the people I must work to love,
Who think of me and see an iron glove.
Here in this huge rehearsal of the past
I dream about that project built to last,
Year zero of the great equality,
The world I'm told there wasn't meant to be,
The world the comrades massed in here betray
By turning up to watch their gods at play.

Vast roar from the **Crowd**. *Blackout.*

Scene Three

The **Crowd** *have all gone, except for the* **Gadgee**, *who stands at the bar (which is also* **Tallow**'*s podium area) with his back to the audience.* **Jackson** *stands centre stage.*

Jackson (*rings on mobile*)
Bobby? Bobby? Where were you? In bed?
You're sick, man, mad like, in the head.
You've gone and missed the fookin Derby game
To shag some bird. Go on, then, what's her name?
Of course you don't. And did you ask her age?
Right. I don't suppose it matters at this stage.

Pause.

Yeah, there with the pee-pel, went to Mass.
They were. We were. We were different class.
Yeah, fucked them Mackems up the arse, yeah –
You can't tell me that sex beats being there.

Pause.

Couple. Rosie's. Forth. The *Telegraph.*
I'm back here now. Come down. We'll have a laugh.

Rings off. Crosses to bar. **Jackson** *emphasises residual Geordie accent speaking to* **Denise**, *the barmaid.*

Excuse me, Miss – a double Bushmill's, please.
Then watch me charm the birdies off the trees.

Denise *serves* **Jackson** (*and, frequently unbidden, keeps the drinks coming at the bar*).

Denise
I never realized you were from round here.

Jackson
Oh aye. The posh wears off when I chase beer.

Gadgee
I knaa you.

Jackson
            Do you?

Gadgee
                        I mean I *knaa you.*

Jackson
Well I don't know you, pal.

Gadgee
                        Howay, you do.

Jackson
If you insist.

Gadgee
            I forgive you. No harm meant.
Fucking great match, man. Not, eh, that I went.
I was busy like. And now – now, I'm pissed.
But not incapable.

Tries to light cigarette, misses, drops cigarette.

                        Ya fuckaz! Missed!

Jackson
Everyone's pissed. It's Saturday night.

Gadgee (*drunken tuneless singing*)
I'm exercising a democratic right.
First I get pissed. Then I fancy a fight.

– I *fancy* a shag but the chances are slight,
So I have to make do.

Finds another cigarette in pocket.

                              Here, man, give us a light.

Jackson (*indicates lighter on counter*)
Help yourself.

Gadgee
I know where I know you from.

Jackson
Yeah?

Gadgee
          You're off the telly, man, am I right?

Jackson (*interested, slightly flattered*)
Maybe.

Gadgee
Am I warm?

Jackson
          Sort of.

Gadgee
                    So I'm warm?

Jackson
                              Boiling.

Gadgee (*triumphantly*)
– You were Tyne Tees weatherman, way back when.

Concerned.
You've lost weight.

Jackson (*shakes head slowly*)
                    James Jackson. Right Hon. MP.
And presently Home Secretary.

Gadgee
Never mind. Tother gadgee must be sick

With always getting took the fookin Mick
By cunts like me mistaking him for ye!
I said I knew you, right? I said. But see,
I'm not sure you're who you're meant to be.
I mean, like, now you're in the government
Are you still our MP, the one we sent?

Jackson
Good question, pal. Can I ask you one back?

Gadgee
Aye, ask us anything. I'm good on Sport.

Jackson (*shakes head*)
It's personal. The question is: what *are* you?
I mean, if who you *are* is what you *do* –

Gadgee
Now you're asking.

Jackson
                        Oh aye, I thought I was.

Gadgee
Why that, though?

Jackson
                        Let's just say *because*.

Gadgee
Seriously?

Jackson
                        Oh gravely. Like the grave.

Gadgee
I'm one of them they didn't try to save.
A man of means by no means, like the song.
I've lost me wife and kids. Me life's all wrong.
But hey, man, what's the point of dwelling on
The world I used to live in? That's long gone,
The lost world, aye, the world called politics:
We fought the law with megaphones and bricks –

And damned if I can still remember why.
The meaning leaves the world as time goes by.

Pause. Begins, more sadly, to sing. Enter **Denise**, *looking anxious.*

I'm just a radgie gadgee on the cadge,
A lonesome cowboy – lost me horse and badge.

Pause. Licks his lips.

Is that enough? I think it is.

Jackson

Not quite.
I might have summat down for you tonight.
Are you a messenger?

Gadgee

How d'ye mean, like?

Jackson
I mean, can you take a message? From me?

Gadgee
Aye, if you want.

Jackson (*to* **Denise**)

Give him a drink.

To **Gadgee**.

I do.

Denise *pours a whisky from the optic.* **Jackson** *gestures that it should be a double.* **Denise** *places it on bar.*

Gadgee
Right. I'm all ears.

Jackson

You are? Come closer, then,

He takes **Gadgee** *in a headlock.*

And listen carefully. Fuck off and die.
Now let me indicate precisely why.

You're old, you're pissed, you're ignorant, you're poor,
The son of a dole-wallah and a hoor.
I've spent my lifetime hoping for the best
From twats like you. You've failed the fuckin test.
You fail at every opportunity.
You fuckin *dare* to fuckin hassle me?
I've half a mind to put you on that floor.
Now do one, cunt, and mind you close the door.

He releases **Gadgee**.

Gadgee
Hey, there's no need for that, son. What I meant –

Jackson
It doesn't fucking *matter* what you meant.
You've got no *anger* left.

Gadgee
                         You think so, eh?
I'll show you fuckin *anger* any day.
I've plenty left for cunts like *ye*, right –

Jackson (*sits on settee*)
Forget it, Grandad. Drink up and goodnight.

Denise
You know you shouldn't come here, Billy, man.
How often have I told you that? Come on.
See if they'll serve you in the Fusilier.

Gadgee (*drinks the whisky*)
I'll have you, cunt. You're full of fuckin nowt.
We put yer in – we'll fuckin put yer out.
I knaa ye, knaad yer fatha's fatha, right –
What's true of them holds true of you – yer shite!

Denise (*coming out from behind the bar*)
Billy! Come on or I'll have to call the polis.
He's too rich and you're too old for this!

Jackson (*rising, and following* **Gadgee** *to the exit*)
Denise, Denise, I *am* the bloody police.

Gadgee (*drinks the whisky off in a slug, then savours the last drop*)
Fookin navy middleweight champion, me, right!
Fookin ave the lotta yer, any fookin night!

Exit **Gadgee**.

Denise (*aside*)
Although it might have spoiled your Saturday,
Perhaps you could have listened anyway?
Old Billy –
He went down at King Arthur's Alamo.
Left there to rot a canny time ago,
They gave up tapping signals on the walls.
They suffocated, drowned, got crushed by falls
And when they got above ground they were dead.
They'd lost their houses. He went off his head
And on the drink, and look – he lived to tell
The tale, now he's no labour left to sell.

To **Jackson**.

He's gone. I'm sorry he disturbed you, sir.

Jackson (*shrugs*)
You seem to be imagining I care.
They'll eat him in the bloody Fusilier.
Two double Bush. I see my friend is here.

Enter **Bobby Brammer** *with* **Miranda**. **Brammer** *joins*
Jackson *at the bar, directing* **Miranda** *to sit on the settee. She*
looks with frank interest at both men, who return her gaze as they talk.

Jackson
Well then, Bobby, what's the score upstairs?

Brammer
You might get wrang. They don't like empty chairs
At lunch when the PM has come to town.
Richard Tallow's sport is tiddlywinks.
He can't stand football. Plus he never drinks.
He says his prayers – and so do all the rest.
I had the monkfish. Christ, it looked depressed.

Jackson
So darling, tell me, is he . . . one of us?

Brammer
Petal, now you're being ridiculous.

Jackson
Where'd you find the tart?

Brammer
                        A bloody Lucky Bag.
She's from the States, like – not yer local slag.
She thinks we're forging international links.

Jackson   I bet that isn't all she bloody thinks.

Brammer *takes* **Miranda** *by the hand, raising her from the settee, displaying her to* **Jackson**. **Miranda** *plays along. She's taken something. As he speaks and acts out their encounter, it become clear that* **Brammer** *has, too.*

Brammer
Just when it seemed that Saturday had died
This lass came strolling down the waterside,
A veritable panther in stilettos,
There among the tarts from Boots and Nettos,
In search of you, she said, and would I mind
Suggesting how at this hour she could find
Her way into your presence? I replied
That I'd be glad to offer her a ride,
My business being, naturally, to vet
All visitors, to check what you might get;
Which she accepted, and we came on foot.

Jackson
That was very delicately put.
Make sure she's not a member of the press,
Though where she'd keep a presscard in that dress
Defies imagining. What other crack?

Brammer
Well, Tallow's office rang. You might ring back.

Enter **Eddie Robson**. **Brammer** *Pauses until he's safely passed towards the bar, then continues.*

They want you 'in the regions', well away
From interviews and telly till the day
It all gans bang. By then it makes no odds
Cause they'll have lost, the stupid fookin sods.
They think they're hard cause once they read *The Prince*:
They couldn't tek a piss except with splints.
Areet, Eddie?

Robson (*approaching*)
                Spare the rod now, Bobby, man.
I'm sure young Richard does the best he can.
Jerusalem was not built overnight.

Brammer
Don't come round here and talk that fuckin shite
Just cause Dicky Tallow tret you to a bite
Off his top table. Man, they knew your price.

Jackson (*sidestepping* **Robson***'s approach*)
Oh, come now, Bobby, that's not very nice.
Eddie's offering wor his sound advice,
Based on thirty years' experience –

Brammer
Of making sure his arsehole fits the fence.

Robson (*on his dignity*)
Times do change, James. We all keep moving on.

Jackson (*joining* **Brammer** *on the settee*)
We must, now our majority has gone
And councillors like you face genocide.

Robson
I think we'll leave the people to decide.
That's my lifelong belief: democracy –

Brammer
As long as it can still afford your fee.

Robson (*finishing his drink*)
You're bitter, Bobby. Don't know how to lose
With dignity. You haven't got a clue.
And since you ask, yes, it was lovely grub.
I'll say goodnight. I'm –

Brammer *and* **Jackson**
                              gannin to the club.

Exit **Robson**.

Brammer
Twat.

Jackson
Yes, but harmless. One from the machine.

Pause. **Jackson** *is studying* **Miranda**.

Brammer
Jacksy man – Elizabeth –

Jackson
                              I'll deal with it.

Brammer
I said you'd call her back, like, in a bit.

Jackson
Did you now?

Brammer
                    She *is* your wife. It's only fair.

Jackson
And that's *your* wife, is it, sat over there,
Revealing that she hasn't dyed her hair?

Brammer
Forget I spoke.

Jackson
                          Besides, man, look, she's just a kid.
She could be yours.

Brammer
                    I know, I know, I did
A bad thing. Let me find a bloody priest.

Jackson
Why, man, finish off your drink at least,
Then introduce me to your little friend.

Brammer
I sometimes think it's you who's round the bend.

Both men rise.

Jackson
But who's to say, as long as I'm in charge?
Now row me out to Cleopatra's barge.

Brammer (*interposing himself*)
Her name's Miranda. But like, she's with wor.

Jackson (*sidestepping* **Brammer**)
Then what d'you want to show her to me for?

Lights fade as the two cross the stage towards **Miranda**.

Scene Four

Cut to: **Elizabeth Jackson** *at her desk, lamplight, chainsmoking,
working on legal papers. On the television BBC News 24 is rerunning
extracts from* **Tallow**'s *speech. The sound is turned down. 'When I
am Laid in Earth' from Purcell's* Dido and Aeneas *is playing in the
background on a CD. Slow fade.*

Elizabeth
I'm forty and a politician's wife,
Which surgically removes the private life.
But being great and good, I work instead
For children who would otherwise be dead
Because they're not from Europe or the States
(Whose economic trends decide the fates
Of millions whom the murderers never meet).

My husband's job's to keep you off the street,
Indoors if possible, a citizen
Who knows what's what and what's allowed and when.
I met him up at Oxford reading Law:
He had me, after dinner, on the floor,
From where we somehow seemed to gravitate
To shoestring work on Ouseburn's worst estate,
Defending the unlucky and the lost
Who otherwise could not have met the cost
Of being skint and ignorant and *there*
In that great capital of disrepair.
I went away. That's it. I went away
To study in the wicked USA,
To show James Jackson that I really could
Survive him, and I came home great and good,
By which time he was on the inside track
For when – or if – the Left came roaring back.
You may have seen my charitable face
Arriving fragrantly in some damn place.
We have no children, have we? But the Cause
Is all we need: the vision, the applause.
The ethics are a problem, there's no doubt,
But only if the facts keep leaking out.

Receives call on mobile phone.

These days I share a bed but sleep alone
And live my dreamlife down the telephone.
My daughter – did I say? – is off her head.
She called to say she wishes she were dead.

She is now speaking to **Miranda**.

No, of course I don't mind if you ring
It's just that I don't think there's anything
That I can do to help you, not until
You choose to act upon your own free will,
To recognise the problem, and to try
To solve it. No. I don't want you to die.
That's the reason I've decided: no more
Money. I know what you want it for.

You say that, every time, and then you say
That I don't love you when I won't give way
And help you kill yourself. I know it's hard.
It's hard for me, you know, because I've barred
Myself from seeing you or helping you unless
You do something to face up to this mess.
Please. Take the steps to get the help you need.
Miss you? I miss you very much indeed.
Miranda, I take twenty years of blame,
But junk, not me, will put you on the game –

Lights slowly fade. Music briefly back up.

Scene Five

Lights up on bar. **Miranda** *is seated on a stool between* **Jackson** *and* **Brammer**. **Denise** *is watching* **Miranda** *with interest.*

Brammer
You're very well equipped, it seems to me.

Jackson
And may I ask which university?

Miranda
Wellesley College. It's my year abroad.

Denise (*aside*)
A broad is right, you little bloody fraud.

Miranda (*moving towards the settee*)
I thought with the election on the way –

Brammer
Actually, pet, it's still too soon to say –

Miranda (*ignoring* **Brammer**, *focused on* **Jackson**)
I'd take the opportunity to see
What the major differences might be
Between the media's impact on campaigns
Back home and over here.

She sits on the settee, expectantly.

Denise (*aside*)
                    A tart with brains –
She's got the big dogs thinking with their dicks
They think she thinks they're talking politics.

Jackson
I'm sure we can arrange to guide you through
The process.

Brammer (*hastening to join her on the settee*)
                    Right, then. I'll look after you.

Jackson (*joining them at his leisure*)
Don't crowd the lady, Bobby. Let her choose
Which means of access she would rather lose –

Indicates himself.

The Minister?

Indicates **Brammer**.

                    The bit of grassroots rough?

Jackson *sits on the other end of the settee. Both men are close enough
for* **Miranda** *to touch.*

Miranda
Well, boys, I'm flattered. It's – it's really tough.
Perhaps I really ought to spread my wings
A little wider, see both ends of things.

Jackson
They say variety's the spice of life.

Brammer
Try telling that to Lizzie – that's his wife.

Laughter.

Enter **Daisy**. *She bristles at the sight of* **Miranda**.

Denise (*aside*)
It almost makes this bloody job worthwhile
To see these Titans clash – I mean bigstyle.

Daisy (*to* **Jackson**)
Is this your niece?

Jackson *stands and joins her.*

Miranda (*to* **Brammer**)
        And this must be the missus.

Brammer (*shakes head, amused despite himself.gestures introduction*)
– Daisy, James's PPS. Daisy, this is –

Miranda
Miranda. No one. How're you doing?

Daisy (*icily*)
Great.

Turns her back on **Miranda**.
Aside to **Jackson**.

      I trust it's Brammer that tart's screwing.

Denise (*aside*)
You cling to influence by your fingernails.
They keep you hanging. Man, it never fails.

Jackson (*to* **Daisy**)
I cross my heart, and hope I do it right:
I haven't laid a hand on her all night,
But as I say, the object of my lust
Is you, exclusively, although I must
Sort out some other business before bed,
And then I'll do the various things I said.

To the group.

Give me an hour, friends, while duty calls.
Feel free to drink the drink and paint the walls.
A minute, Bobby. Walk me to the door,
Then show these ladies what the night is for.

Exit **Jackson** *and* **Brammer**.

Denise (*aside*)
Which leaves the floor to bitches A and B.

You don't get stuff like this on BBC.

Miranda
You look *tired*, girl.

Daisy (*going to the bar*)
                    And you look cheap.

Miranda
You ought to go and get a good night's sleep.

Daisy
You ought to go and sell it on the street.

Miranda (*rising and joining* **Daisy**)
You're frightened, right, because you can't compete?
But look, don't worry. It's a one-time thing.
Hey, Daisy, in the meantime, wanna swing?

Daisy (*shivers, appalled at this impertinence*)
Just drink your drink and meet the tiny stars
You meet if you just hang around in bars,
But don't suppose there'll really be a place
In this world for your coked-out little face.
While he

Indicating **Brammer**.

            may call on you for certain acts,
He'll flush you down like Durex. Face the facts.

Holds out money to **Miranda**.

Don't let me find you here –

Miranda
                        when you get back?
Or what?

A switchblade is suddenly there and open in **Miranda**'s *hand.*

            You wanna leave the party in a sack?

*The music has changed now to Ry Cooder's 'That's the Way the Girls
are from Texas', which plays over the fading lights.*

Scene Six

Elizabeth's *study. she leans on the desk, smoking.* **Jackson** *enters unnoticed. Even the angriest passages in this scene should reveal the attraction and affection* **Elizabeth** *and* **Jackson** *have for each other.*

Jackson
You know you want to give the tabs up, pet.

Elizabeth
Who said, 'Please make me good but not just yet'?

Jackson
St Augustine.

They embrace and kiss. **Elizabeth** *moves a little apart.*

I've missed you. Been a while.

Elizabeth
I thought that married life was out of style.

Jackson
Form's temporary, Lizzie; class remains.

Elizabeth
And Daisy Gates? The blonde with shit for brains?

Jackson
Just duvet candy, Lizzie. You know me,
That what you get's not always what you see –

Elizabeth
I do indeed. I know you're talking shite.

Jackson
Then give me chance –

Elizabeth
                    I know: to put it right.
And this is class, is it? A midnight kiss?
Life has to be more difficult than this.

Jackson
Of course it does. But not inside this room.

From here I could ignore the crack of doom.
Although we're rowing, here at least I get
An hour –

Elizabeth
            – to talk about yourself. It's sad:
When they gave out the pronouns you were had.
You travel fluently from 'I' to 'we'
But find it hard to grasp the point of

Indicates herself.

                                         'me',
Or 'her' as I'd be called in Daisy's bed.

Jackson *turns away, mortified.*

Elizabeth
Forgive me, Jacksy. Something that I said?
But while you . . . conjugate, I must decline
Your invitation. I won't stand in line.

Pause.

Listen, James, we have to clear the slate
Before long, or admit that it's too late.
I'm much too old for waiting by the phone
And loyally spending all my nights alone –

Jackson
That's it. There's someone else.

Elizabeth
                              That's rich.
I'm Caesar's wife, so when you feel an itch
You want to scratch, you blame biology,
But somehow this does not apply to me.

Jackson
Who is it?

Elizabeth
No one.

Jackson
                    Is it William Farr?
For fucksake, girl, he's married to the bar!

Elizabeth
I promise you, you'll be the first to know.
Oh, this is useless, James. Just go.

Jackson
Lizzie, look, I want to put it right.

Elizabeth
                              You've said.
I don't just want lip-service in my bed
But every inch of you committed to
The work we always said we had to do.

Jackson
Such as?

Elizabeth
          You don't remember? Fine. Good night.
Our language was abolished by the Right.
Equality? It must be infantile
If it won't spread its legs and think of style.

Jackson
You must see how the world is not the same
As when we kicked off in the this bloody game.
There's not an inch, a toehold anywhere –

Elizabeth
And therefore – let me finish – we won't care?

Jackson (*shrugs*)
It's winter. We adapt. We camouflage.

Elizabeth
But don't you simply want to be in charge?
These mad, inverted principles that you've
Somehow got saddled with – to me they prove
You've missed the entrance to your bloody life –
And that's where I live. I'm your bloody wife!

Now you've determined that it's you alone
Who listens in when Britain's on the phone.
You wield the apparatus of the State
As if you think your second name is fate.
I wonder you're not bugging people's dreams.

Jackson (*bitterly amused*)
That's first among my post-election schemes.

Elizabeth
Marx never got elected, did he, James?
And all you're playing now is graveyard games,
Three times around the tomb and back, in case
Das Kapital comes true. You've lost your place.

Jackson
Just let me get the campaign over, right?
Then I'm at your disposal every night
And when we're tired we'll make policy.

Elizabeth
Aha. And when d'you say that's going to be?

Jackson
Six weeks.

Elizabeth
Till then. I'll hold you to this pledge.

Jackson
Till then.

Exit **Jackson**.

Elizabeth
            Now there's a boy who's near the edge
And one who'd rather die than compromise.
Do I believe him and his big blue eyes?
I'd *better*.
It's sad, though. I preferred the two of us
When we were foolish and anonymous
Campaigners for – can you remember what?
But we were young. Apparently we were.
Whatever youth might be, we left it there.

She raises her glass.

A toast! The wrong end of the telescope
Shows tiny children in the days of hope.

She drinks.

And all those years ago I walked away.
What brought me back? And now what makes me stay?
Well . . . let me tell you how I theorise
About my life, then tell me if it's lies.
A partnership of principle outlives
Mere human error: partnership forgives
And keeps itself in view. An act of will
Can be as tender as a kiss. I still
Believe that – on my better days I do.
Equality. I still believe in that. Do you?
So now, James, when your chance is almost here,
I won't embarrass you, or disappear.
I'll be, like Auden, the more loving one,
Until that chance is taken, or it's gone.
Till then I'm back inside my padded cell,
With my mad child, and no one I can tell.

Music back up as lights fade.

Scene Seven

Enter **Farr**, *by now a bit drunk. He carries a copy of the*
Guardian. **Denise** *is polishing glasses behind the bar.*

Farr (*sings, in the voice of an Irish tenor*)
Beer and tabs my only hobbies are,
I would go home again but it's too far,
So constable direct me to the bar.

Notices **Denise**.

Pint of Scotch and a geet large Grouse, please, pet.
Bit quiet, innit. Still, it's early yet.

Denise
It's always like this now on Saturday.
There's only drunks and ghosts come out to play
– And sometimes politicians on the town.
That lot want to drink until they drown.

Farr
And which am I?

Denise
                    It's hard to tell, although
Dead men don't drink Scotch, as far as I know.

Farr
Depends exactly what you mean by dead –
I'm still alive, but all my say's been said.
Oh, I'm still sort of standing, more or less,
Although because I'm honest I confess
I've supped some stuff and seen the Pearly Gate
At closing time. St Peter said: 'You're late.
And anyway, we don't let poets in:
We find they tempt the virgins here to sin.'

Denise
Poets? Are you saying you're a poet?

Farr
                                        Was.

Toasts himself.

I sacrificed myself in that great cause.
And do my penance at the university
Teaching kids who'll none of them read me –
Nor, come to that, whatever makes them think.
You know the rest. Failed poet = drink.
I had the gift, the publisher, the wife,
But all of that was far too much like life.

Denise
I wrote a poem once.

Farr
                        You did. Of course.

Denise
All about this lad.

Farr
                    Of course you did, of course.
Just like your nearly book, your almost horse.

Denise
He was a bastard.

Farr
The Greek, Arkilokos, once wrote some stuff –
Because his bitchy girlfriend cut up rough –
That drove not just the girl but mother too
To suicide. That might appeal to you,
A poem which is art and yet a curse.

Denise
I showed mine to my teacher. She'd read worse
But said my style was well, like, out of date –
Besides, he'd shagged my friend by then. Too late.
But poetry? – it's always been that way
And fuck-all use to barmaids anyway.
These poems you once wrote: so did they rhyme?

Farr
When I remembered. When I found the time.

Denise
Is it just poems you write, or proper books?

Farr (*aside*)
With brains like yours be thankful for your looks.

Denise
Pardon?

Farr
         Nowt, love. Just stick a big Black Bush in there,
As Rimbaud once remarked to Baudelaire,
Who felt the wing of madness brushing past.
Now drink up, Farr. Your next might be your last.

Farr *sits on the settee. Enter* **Jackson** *with* **Brammer**.

Jackson
Remember, after this I'm not around.

Brammer
I've no idea where you've gone to ground.
No matter who calls?

Jackson
                    Sure you understand?
All right. Let's piss the night away as planned.

Brammer *rolls his eyes in mock exhaustion.*

Brammer
Er, what about Miranda? She looked fit.

Jackson
You want to tie a bloody knot in it.

Brammer
Well anyway, I need a fuckin piss.

Jackson
Well, be my guest.

Exit **Brammer**.

Jackson *sees* **Farr**. *In the following passage the men speak with the heavy, joshing irony of once-firm friends groping – despite their aggression – for a point of contact.*

                    Now then, now then, who's this?
I seem to recognise that purple face,
The tiny tremor of the hopeless case,
The paper open at the crossword page.
You've missed a clue: it's *act your age*.
No use to one who still believes he's Keats,
Who drinks the vintage clear but never eats.
William Farr, the bard of bed and beer –
So what the fuck are you still doing here?

Farr
I live here. You?

Jackson

It's Conference time.

Farr

I saw your speech somewhere. Wage war on crime,
That it? The kind of pixilated shite
We formerly expected from the Right,
But now the People's Party's been reborn –

Jackson

My policies give Widdecombe the horn.
That's politics. But I'm on holiday
From now till Sunday morning, miles away
From ideology and suchlike ills.

Notices that **Farr** *is swallowing tablets. Takes the prescription bottle from him.*

Should you be drinking if you're on those pills?

Farr (*snatching the bottle back*)
Do I tell you how crime should be prevented?
I take these pills or else I go demented.
It's my life's work, these days, is being ill,
And so my badge of office is this pill.

Swallows it with whisky.

That's the kind of bargain that you strike
When what you want's too much of what you like.
You might escape from ideology
But I'm convinced that that's what did for me,
Watching you sell Labour down the river –

Jackson

– justifies the damage to your liver.
I've heard 'em, every Militant excuse –
But face it, you were just no bloody use
Except of course when you were writing verse:
It does fuck all but doesn't make things worse.
But let's not argue now. We've got all night.

Farr (*rising, going to the bar*)

Large Talisker, third optic on the right.
So Tallow thinks it's time: let England choose.
A bad mistake. Because *this* time you'll lose.
But then, of course, this is democracy.

Jackson

Exactly, and the people must be free
To put their money on the other gang
Although their headline policy's to hang
Left-footers, nonces, queers and Micks and blacks
In numbers. And what else? They can't cut tax.
Remember how round here folk used to say
They'd vote a chimpanzee in just as long
As it was Labour?

Farr

                    Who says they were wrong?

Jackson

My point exactly. Bless 'em, all the Neds,
Who sleep like socialists in king-size beds
But wake up every day like Tamburlaine,
Especially if Blue House is blocked again.

Laughs. Phone rings.

Farr

His Master's voice, eh?

Jackson (*lightly, to* **Farr**)

                    Fuck you too.

Into telephone.

Not now, Bobby. Look, man, I just said
To tell 'em anything. Just say I'm dead.
I see. Oh yes, that's marvellous. Oh shit.
Right, Bobby, right. Just let me deal with it.

To **Farr**.

That's just the world. It won't let me alone.

To **Denise**.

Don't let our local poet buy his own.

Jackson *moves slightly apart into the 'outside'/bridge/quayside area. To make call. lights up on* **Tallow** *in upstage 'office' area with* **Glass** *and* **Daisy Gates**.

Tallow (*menacing calm*)
We've run into a local problem, James.
So let's not muck around. You know these names?
A councillor called Robson? Ouseburn Club?
You sound as if you're standing in a pub.

Jackson
I came in for a couple from the match.
Give me those names again. I didn't catch –

Tallow
Look, our man on the *Sun* contacted us.
There's been a whisper, still anonymous,
But Gregor's found out who it has to be
Who plans to drop you in it royally.
Ouseburn Club? Some council drone called Robson?
The shit just hit the fan. The shit's got knobs on.
It's seem he thinks the papers will be keen
To hear his tale –

Jackson (*laughs*)
Robson? Eddie Robson? What's he said?
I thought somebody told me he was dead.

Tallow
Quite possibly, but what concerns me more
Is whether he'll make trouble and who for.
He says ten years ago a rigged committee
Sold council land to interests in the city –
Prime sites for those who like to speculate,
Delivered, for a kickback, on a plate –
And Ouseburn Club, it seems, was one such place –
Arranged, he says, by such a well-known face
That every tabloid worth its tits would kill
For half a chance to be the first to spill

The business steaming in the nation's lap –
Which *simply cannot happen*, right, old chap?
I'm handing you to Gregor Glass now, James;
Just give him all the numbers and the names.
And think of what a pity it would be
If scandal came between yourself and me –
We've six weeks till the nation goes to vote:
Mess that up and I'll cut your fucking throat.

Hands over phone to **Glass**. *Exit* **Tallow**.

Glass
Good evening, James. I trust I find you well,
Despite the sudden all-prevailing smell
That emanates from the unburied past.
Has Jacksy dropped a bollock at long last?

Jackson
Thanks. Not just now, you little Tartan queer.

Hangs up. Rings **Brammer**.

Oh, Bobby? I need Daisy over here.
The Pit Bar. Next door to the Quay.
She tells no one the call has come from me.
And, Bobby. Find me Eddie. I don't care:
If he's in Durham nick, then find him there.
And if you see that little bastard Glass
Then shove a red-hot poker up his arse.

Lights down on **Jackson**. *Up on* **Glass** *and* **Daisy**.

Glass
Needless to say it's not our present goal
To save the Minister's immortal soul.

Daisy
I know, I know: observe and then report
How deeply in the mire our friend is caught.
Although he really is a beast in bed,
A girl can't go on sleeping with the dead.

Exeunt **Glass** *and* **Daisy**. *Lights up on* **Farr** *and* **Jackson** *on settee.*

Farr
So where's Elizabeth?

Jackson
                    Who wants to know?

Farr
Somehow I just imagined she'd be here.

Jackson
She's never been that keen on tabs and beer.

Farr
She might mind –

Jackson
                    – if she knew I played away?
Could that be what you're struggling to say?
I doubt it. Anyway, of course, she knows
I mix her poetry with rougher prose.
Forget it, William. It's understood,
And nothing you can say'll do any good.

Farr
It's middle age. It scares me, Jacksy man –
And thus

Indicates his glass. Stands up.

          I'll die as quickly as I can.
See, I remember, I remember when–

Jackson
Of course you do. But don't start that again.
How you and I were solidarity
Itself and damn the brain-dead NEC
And our impassioned programme for the cause
Would wake up Marx to lead the world's applause.
Back when we could sleep on floors and screw
The sisterhood and frame the world anew –

Those were the days when we were young and daft.
Well our ship sank, and I got on the raft.
I've not forgotten – I just don't believe . . .
In wearing old commitments on my sleeve.

Approaches **Farr**.

The people you believe in – they're all dead;
The live ones get bought off with garlic bread,
Cheap wine and fancy knickers for the wife –
The Metro Centre stands in place of strife.

Farr
I only asked.

Jackson
        Can Socialism live?
Well, only if it's fucking punitive –
Like Walter Ulbricht learned at Stalin's feet:
Feed 'em, clothe 'em, keep 'em off the street.
And make 'em understand whose fault it is
If life consists of such austerities.

Farr
You can't just *hate* the folk you represent.

Jackson (*laughs*)
Not all, man, just the rotten element.
You have to be objective in the end –
A lesson you could never learn, old friend.

Farr
You're mad.

Jackson
        The second time someone's said that.
Well, watch out, lumpenproletariat.

Act Two

Scene One

Enter **Eddie Robson** *and* **Woman**. *Both are drunk. they have stepped out of a club bar, the noise of which can be heard in the background, plus bass/drums of music inside, which turns out fleetingly to be 'Things Can Only Get Better'. Occasional flickers of disco light.*

Woman

Eee, Cooncillor Robson, I'm married, me –
You'd best not let me bloody husband see.
He's dead jealous, specially when he's pissed –
He maimed this lad the last time I got kissed.

Robson

He'll not see owt. I've left him full of drink
Sat in the bog asleep. You didn't think
I bought him all those rounds because I *like*
The cunt? I'm after borrowing his bike.

Woman

You've got a silver tongue, I'll give you that.

Robson

Aye, that's not all. You want to see me flat.
It's got like a jacuzzi plus a bed
So big there's bits I haven't visited.
Perhaps you'd fancy playing hide-and-seek
Before we do the business, so to speak.

Woman

Well, it's tempting. I don't mind admitting
I'm a sucker for expensive fittings.
But I dunno. 'Cos I've had nowt to eat.
Stop *doing* that! We're in the public street.

Robson

I've got some lovely sausage.

Woman

So I see.
But do you think you're man enough for me?

Enter **Brammer** *and* **Heavy**.

Brammer
Well, pet, you won't be finding out tonight.
Besides, you're Davy Dillon's missus, right?

Woman
What's it to do with you?

Heavy *takes her by the arm.*

Brammer

I'm Davy's mate.
Time's getting on. So put your lipstick straight
And we'll forget that you were here. OK?

Robson
Now hang on –

Brammer

Make him understand.

Heavy *punches* **Robson** *in the stomach. He goes down on his
knees, winded.*

Brammer

Howay,
It's business, love, between us and

Prods **Robson** *with his foot.*

this shite,
The sort of thing that might take us all night . . .
So, as you see, it's time to slip away
And put yourself about another day.

Kisses her roughly.

I'll not say owt, of course, and nor will you.
Next time don't pick a cooncillor to screw.

Brammer *slaps her backside. She screams and exits running.*
Heavy *hauls* **Robson** *to his feet.*

Well now, who's been a greedy little get?
Come on. We've hardly started on you yet.

Exeunt. Blackout.

Scene Two

*By lighting, indicate that this bar is a basement, somewhere 'below' the
bar in Act One.*

Enter **Jackson**. *Mobile phone.*

Jackson
Bobby – have you found him? Brilliant. Great.
Bring him down here then. Use the basement gate.
Anyway, where was he? Club? Yeah? *Shiremoor*?
So what's he want to go to *that* dump for?
The one place left he still might get his hole.
Well, bring him in – we'll stop his rigmarole.

Hangs up. Enter **Daisy**.

We're going to have to face a lot of press –
I've got dragged into some old local mess,
So what I want's a statement –

Daisy
                        Well, hello.
What happened to the Jacksy who, you know,
Was all for nailing Daisy to the bed.
Can it have been something that Daisy said?

Jackson
By no means, Daisy. There's a hitch, that's all.
I nail that, or I'm up against the wall.

Daisy
Oh, Jacksy, Jacksy, Daisy understands.
The media will find work for idle hands.
The jealous failures, stuck here in the sticks,

Feed whispers to the tabloids for their kicks –
A name, a date, a polaroid or two –
You see that bloke in bondage – well, it's you.
So then the broadsheets gravely speculate
On what it means, and then it's far too late
To plug the dyke or stop the stinking tide.
And worst of all it helps the other side.
Six weeks before the Neds go out to vote.
Six weeks: the Party has to stay afloat.

Pause.

In view of which, Miranda's lousy news.
She might suggest she wants to 'learn your views',
But that's not what that scrubber has in mind.

Jackson
Forget it, Daisy, OK? I'm not blind.
She's just a moth who likes to feel the flame,
That's all.

Daisy
            A *moth*? She's on the bloody game.

Jackson
Oh, Daisy, look, do I go short of sex?
A Secretary of State can't drop his kex
Like other blokes indulging normal lust,
Unless his squeeze is someone he can trust.

Embraces her.

And you remain my premier odalisque,
Which leaves the Glassman as the major risk,
So now, what is it you've already heard?
Who told you then? A little bastard bird?

Daisy
A tiny whisper in the corridors –

Jackson
The kind of thing that's overheard by whores?

Squeezes her roughly.

Daisy
The kind of thing, Jacksy, you pay me for.
That's why I have to talk to Gregor Glass –

Jackson (*releases her, as though disgusted*)
Who's saving Labour for the middle class.
He thinks the world's a sodding Oxford quad.

Daisy (*mimics* **Jackson**)
– The sort that even snubs Almighty God . . .
Just tell me what you want. A statement, right?
That doesn't have to take all bloody night.

Jackson
This Robson knacker reckons he can prove
That – years ago – I rubberstamped a move
To sell off Ouseburn Club for building land.

Daisy
And did you?

Jackson
                    Yes, but not for cash in hand.
That's why *he* would have done it, any day,
And pissed it all back into Whitley Bay.
But it was Harry Black's retirement plan –
Old Council Leader, lifelong union man –
Director of this building firm, you see,
Who said he'd pass the Party on to me
If I'd just see him and the wife all right,
And so I did. And thank you and good night.
What was it, after all? Some crap old club
For gadgees. Let them use the fucking pub.
I oiled the wheels. And I was right, OK?

Daisy
James, you know how this is going to play
If there's a sniff. You'll end up crucified.
Why not retaliate first? Try suicide.

Jackson
All this was years ago. It doesn't count.

Daisy

What's Tallow's riff? 'The fact, not the amount
Is how we have to judge a case of sleaze.
We do not sympathise with a disease.'
You know you scare him. This would be his chance
To prove that's not a clothes peg down his pants.
Imagine: you're the enemy within –
For Tallow that could just supply a win:
Tough on sleaze and tougher on its cause.
Cue lights, cue camera, cue vast applause.

Jackson

But I brought jobs to Ouseburn when that word
Was something people's grandfathers had heard;
Real jobs, that made things we could really sell –

Daisy

And Ouseburn made you its MP as well.
From where you rose to Cabinet and fame.
Spare me. It all just sounds the bloody same.
Remember that the language of tradition
Means fuck all to girls in my position
I hope you're not expecting me to weep.
So what about this . . . Eddie Robson creep?

Jackson *takes hold of her arm. Slight menace.*

Jackson

Leave that to me. Just have a statement ready:
Flat denial. Now then: here comes Eddie.

Enter **Robson** *with* **Brammer** *and* **Heavy**. **Robson** *has his
hands tied behind his back and a handkerchief stuck in his mouth.*

Excuse us, Daisy. This could be a mess.

Exit **Daisy**.

Evening, Eddie. Something to confess?

Removes handkerchief from **Robson**'s *mouth.*

Brammer
Seems coitus fuckin interruptus here
's a hard man, right? A cunt who knows no fear.

Robson
I don't know where you get off doing this.
Fuckin bouncers, Jacksy? Divvent tek the piss.

Heavy *punches* **Robson** *in the face. He yells and falls. Enter, unnoticed,* **Farr**.

Jackson (*kneeling by the prone* **Robson**)
I can't recall that you were ever shy
When time came for letting folk know why
They shouldn't scab or strike or jump
The wrong way round the bloody Parish pump.

Rises, indicating to **Heavy** *to get* **Robson** *to his feet.*

You were always handy with your fists:
It's thanks to you this . . . policy . . . exists.

Robson
At least I did me dirty work meself.

Jackson
But now you're only doing it for pelf.

Heavy punches **Robson** *in the face. He falls, now bleeding from the mouth.*

Jackson
So tell me, comrade, why's it take so long
For you to try to sell me for a song?
Bear in mind by morning you'll retract,
Right, Eddie? Please, account for this strange act.

Robson
Tell your gorillas this is where it stops.
Or else when I leave here I'll call the cops.

Brammer
What makes you think you're going anywhere?

Robson
You cross-eyed cunt, you wouldn't fookin dare.

Brammer
Heavy – get the bucket and the hammer.

He throws **Robson** *on to the settee. Sits next to him, stroking his hair.*

This smart twat's annoying Bobby Brammer.

Exit **Heavy**.

Jackson
Why'd you do it, Eddie?

Robson (*now terrified*)
                    Like you said,
For cash. To take me daughter to the States,
For treatment that you can't get on the rates –
Expensive business, cancer of the bone.
I couldn't manage that lot on me own.
She'll die of waiting for the NHS –
If you had kids you'd not do any less.
If I can make a tabloid write a cheque
For seven grand, of course I'll risk me neck.

Jackson
I still can't let you sell me to the press.
I'll have to ruin you instead. Oh, yes,
I know your history of little deals,

With cartoon swagger.

Cause I'm the wheel that turns the other wheels –
Including yours, you humble democrat.
It's in the book, you little alky twat.

Brammer
It's not just tarts and dinner, man, it's fraud.
That ought to stop the jury getting bored.

Robson
Howay –

Jackson
      – Howay yourself.

Enter **Heavy** *with bucket of water and a hammer.*

Robson
                              Aw, Jacksy, man.

Brammer
You know he'll do it, Eddie, cause he can.
'A politician sweeps his own backyard.'
The press like that. It keeps the image hard.
New Labour takes a very serious view
Of felonies by Party men like you.
Remember Jack's Home Secretary as well:
You'll do hard time in HM Prison, Hell –
And how's it going to help to heal the sick
If you spend six years sucking someone's dick?

Jackson
But do things really have to go that far?
You've not yet told the paper who you are?
And your anonymous contact – that was made
To see how much you'd end up getting paid?
So no one really knows but me and thee
And Bobby here, who won't be saying, see,
So how about I give you what you need
And you go home, keep very shtum indeed,
Forget we met, just pay the doctor's bill.

Robson
I only did it 'cos she's really ill.

Jackson
So you said. And I can understand.

Brammer *helps* **Robson** *to his feet.* **Jackson** *unties him and throws the rope to* **Heavy**.

Jackson
What happens now is, first, I shake your hand,
Then Bobby takes you quickly to the bank

And all of us have common sense to thank
For not allowing problems we can fix
To ruin us with leaks to tabloid pricks.
Bobby, Heavy, please escort our friend
To his reward. This matter's at an end.

Exeunt **Brammer**, *leading the confused* **Robson** *by the hand,*
followed by **Heavy**, *who is still carrying the hammer and the bucket*
of water.

Farr (*coming centre stage*)
I daresay that was realpolitik.

Jackson
Are you still there? You never heard a squeak.

Farr
Man, you never could tell right from wrong.
When we went up against the National Front
That time, you fucking crippled that poor cunt.

Jackson (*brightening*)
That wasn't business, William, that was fun.
You may recall he also had a gun
When all we had was theory and fists:
You meet the situation that exists.
I ought to make a move. With any luck
Before I fall asleep I'll get a fuck.

Farr
One question, though. Of all the things to be
Why did you choose Home Secretary?

Jackson
Because he owns the armies of the night.
Unarguably on the Party's right,
His is the most consistently reviled
Of all the Offices of State. When Howard smiled
Or Straw gave glib offence to Parliament
All liberal hearts knew what their presence meant:
That soon the State's enforcers would be sent
So slaughter of the first-born could begin.

The *Daily Mail* is where you have to win.
Judge and jury, grass and executioner:
Jack's not political; he's simply there.
Besides, like Lucifer, I studied law.
What else should I have bored my arse off for?

Enter **Daisy**.

Daisy
I've brought a draft you may just want to read.

Jackson
File it. Now it doesn't seem we'll need
To brief the Press tonight. But Daisy, thanks
For helping clear my lawn of Tallow's tanks.
And this is an old friend, right? William Farr's –

Daisy
– The subject of a hundred seminars.
At Oxford we all agonised for days
About your early work, though not the plays.
What was it? Oh, yes, ambiguity.
You're not how I'd imagined you would be.
For one thing, really, shouldn't you be dead?

Farr
You're very sweet to one no longer read.
These days I like to sit round and observe
The conduct of those paragons who serve
Our interests in the parliamentary sphere.
So tell me – Daisy? – what brings you in here?
A girl like you with your patrician mouth
Seems to belong somewhere much further south.

Daisy
Oh, class is dead, like dodos – or like verse.

Farr
They just forgot to load me on the hearse.
I like her. True, the ignorance appals.
But never mind. She's certainly got balls.

Jackson
Ignore him, Daisy. William's only drunk –

Daisy
As men become when they run out of spunk.
You're sure there's nothing else?

Jackson
                                    I'll join you, right?

Daisy
It looks as if you're in for quite a night.

Jackson
By the way, let Master Gregor know . . .
That if he tries to have another go
At winding up Big Jack the Hanging Judge.
Then one night when he stays home packing fudge
I'll tear his Jambo head off, then I'll piss
Inside his heart. Hang on. Come here. Big kiss.

Jackson *makes sure that* **Farr** *sees this is for his benefit. Exit* **Daisy**. *Lights down.*

Scene Three

Sound of dripping water as under bridge. Lights like reflections of water. Sound of car approaching and stopping, cars doors slamming.

Enter **Brammer** *and* **Robson**. **Robson** *is visibly drunk now.* **Brammer** *carries a bottle of Scotch.*

Brammer
Now then, Eddie marrer. Get this down yer.

Robson *(finding it all amusing)*
So have yer brought us here to drown wor?
Eh, Jacksy said to tek us to the bank.

Hugely amused. Drinks.

Brammer *(playing along with drunkenness but not drunk)*

Aye. Jacksy said to bring you to the bank.
Whatever happens, you've got him to thank.
Least said and soonest mended – so they say.
'Course, that's not how I'd handle scabs. No way.
I've got some geet imaginative schemes,
The sort of stuff you do to folk in dreams.
Be grateful, cunt, it's not just down to me
We're here at dead of night. 'Cos then we'd see.

Robson (*drinks, grows maudlin*)
One time we was mates, like, you and me.
I suppose you think that's all just history.
Watter underneath the bridge and that.
You think I'm bent? Well, all I've got's a flat,
Two suits, a dodgy liver and the past.
And memory, of course. But that won't last.
I'm not a thinker. I don't understand.
Why's it not worked out the way we planned?
We've stood on picket lines and had the shit
Kicked out of us and didn't care a bit
Because the cause was right. Remember that.

Brammer
Don't you dare get sentimental, twat.

Robson
D'you hate me cause I let meself be bought?

Brammer
Can't say I've give it that much thought.
You're just another arsehole on the grab,
A traitor, bosses' lackey, secret scab,
And all them other names we used to call
The common enemy when we was all
Still singing out in blood-red harmony.
And nowadays? you don't mean shite to me.
But I can tell you've summat else to say.
Go on, then, Eddie. Get it out the way.

Robson
It's – see, I lied.

Brammer

Well I never.

Robson

Aye, I did.

Brammer

Well, what about, like?

Robson

It's, well, our kid –

Brammer

You've never made it up that she was bad?

Robson

No, Bobby, man. I almost wish I had
She's sick, all right. She needs the operation.
It's just, like, who I gave the information.

Brammer

You what? You said you gave it to the *Sun*.

Robson

The journalist, OK? There wasn't one.

Brammer

Who was it then?

Pause.

Fuck me. That bastard Glass.

Robson

Somehow he'd got to hear about our lass.
He said it was a problem we could fix
If I'd just help him pull one of his tricks.
He reckoned Jacksy'd have to take the bait.

Brammer

And does Glass know yet?

Robson (*shakes head*)

Thought I'd better wait
Until I'd seen the money.

Brammer
                        That makes sense.
That's clever, right. You're both sides of the fence.

Robson
I only did it for the lass.

Brammer
                        Why aye, man.
We've all to try and do the best we can.
Oi, Heavy, time we saw old Eddie right.

Enter **Heavy** *with bucket and hammer and upright chair. And wearing a butcher's apron. Sets down bucket.*

Robson
Where's me money?

Heavy *smashes* **Robson** *in the knee. He falls, screaming.* **Heavy** *continues to belabour him, then ties* **Robson***'s hands behind his back.*

Brammer
                        What money, you soft shite?
It's been decided by the management
To confiscate your prize in lieu of rent –
Your six-foot plot's somewhere beneath the Tyne.
I saw this film where someone drowned in wine,
Some Shakespeare that we watched at school one day,
Supposed to help us understand the play.
I never could get on with poetry,
But murderology? It worked for me.
Now, I'm afraid we've got no Beaujolais,
But Scotch'll do to drown you in. Howay.

Brammer *and* **Heavy** *push* **Robson***'s head into the bucket and hold it there while* **Robson** *struggles. They let him up for a breath, then shove him under again. Blackout.*

Act Three

Scene One

*Music, briefly: Brecht/Eisler's 'Hollywood Elegy No. 7', sung by
Matthias Goerne. Sound of trains over bridges, church clocks striking.
Lights up on* **Farr**, *who is by now very drunk and sitting on the back
of the settee. He begins to declaim.* **Denise**, *also on the settee, is
listening.*

Farr

Your hundred streets, your twenty names, all gone.
A stink of burning sofas in the rain,
Of pissed-on mattresses, and poverty's
Spilt milk in tiny airless rooms designed
To illustrate the nature of subjection
To its subjects. They say that this age lacks
A project for its politics: here's grease
Extruded from the dripping tar-skinned walls
Of working-men's hotels; the ropes of hair
Trapped in the sinks; the names perpetually denied
A hearing, waiting in the smoky halls
For their appointments with an age that bred
And killed and then forgot them – names that now
Forget themselves, the air's mere allegations,
Faces that the mirrors do not hold,
Lockers with no contents, neither razors
Nor the Bible nor an envelope of dimps
Preserved against the certainty of worse.
So Billy, Tommy, Jackie – did you live?
Could it be you that Benjamin's
Averted angel is ignoring now
As once again you leave your flooded graves
Like newsreel ghosts to greet the Kaiser's guns?

Enter **Jackson**.

Jackson

Iceland, Luxembourg and Spain: *nul points*.

Denise *resumes her place at the bar.*

Farr
The times the poet lives in won't anoint
The work for which he makes his sacrifice.
If there was any justice I'd live twice.
Instead I'm dying on my arse in here.

Jackson
Waitress, bring this poet extra beer.

Denise
Excuse me, sir, I'm not sure if I can.
He's drunk enough to kill a normal man.

Farr
Well, I'm not normal, am I? I'm a bard.
They think we're soft. See me, pet, I'm geet hard.
So serve me beer pursued by uisgebaugh.

Jackson
This is the famous poet, William Farr.

Denise
It's no use being famous when you're dead.
How'd you know your stuff was even read?

Farr
Although she's not as stylish as I am,
I like Denise. She gives good epigram.
The sort of girl you want to dedicate
A poem to before it gets too late,
So she'll perhaps remember me at least
When I'm a spectre absent from the feast.
She's more than individual, this lass –
She can exemplify a dying class.
So that was one for all you serving girls
Who have to warm their mistress' ropes of pearls.
To all of you, from all us hierophants.

Denise (*aside*)
He thinks that this'll get him in me pants.

Jackson
Now then, Denise, so what d'you make of that
Performance? Is he genius or twat?
Or was it hard for you to understand
The failure of the future we had planned?
Think about it while I have a piss.

To **Farr**.

I must admit I'm quite enjoying this.

Exit **Jackson**.

Denise
A poem for me? I couldn't really tell.

Farr
Denise, I mean: we've died and this is Hell.
Here's all that's left of socialism, pet –
It's gone but hasn't even happened yet.
The world we dreamed of died before your time.
– You may have noticed that one didn't rhyme.

Denise
I'll mebbes get the sack now, Mr Farr,
But do you know how privileged you are?
To stand here all night propping up the bar
And holding forth with all your politics
While someone else is mopping up your sick's
A pretty cushy number, isn't it?

Farr
Correct. But later on I'll feel like shit.
I'm storing up the guilt. It's what I use
To work. But darling, please continue to abuse
My self-indulgent, snobbish motormouth.
Denise. You stir me deeply, way down south.

Farr *sits down heavily. He falls asleep.*

Denise (*to the sleeping* **Farr**, *as she takes his glass from his hand
and tidies up around him*)
'The poor man's nerve-tic, irony':

Can that apply to workie cows like me?
The line's from Louis Simpson: know his stuff?
His sympathy's with those who have it rough.
I read him when I slogged through my degree –
Three years for sweet fuck all if you ask me –
But, Mr Farr, I'm hazarding a guess
You share, not just the verse, but an address
Where you don't have to hear the hours I keep.
My working life takes place while you're asleep
Or drunk, and when by chance we intersect
You wouldn't mind, were I to genuflect.
I keep my temper, work and feed my kid –
A sight more than her father ever did.
Oh, once upon a time the likes of me
Made furniture in plants in Peterlee
And Stanley. We were living in the past.
The ground beneath our feet seemed built to last
And there were unions to protect us, even then,
Against the plans of offshore money men,
So when we went on strike we all supposed
We'd go official, get the factory closed
And force the bosses to negotiate.
They brought in scabs who undercut our rate,
The union claimed its fucking hands were tied,
And our MP passed on the other side
In his red Volvo, weekends when he came
To show his face and watch the fucking game,
Glassed in on high with those who locked us out.
So is that what your poems are about?
I've shat the sort of socialist you are
But I still have to serve you at the bar.
The poet Farr, in thrall to the profound?
He'll kiss yer arse if you can buy a round,
Then bite the hand that feeds the vulture sat
To eat his liver. He's confused, poor twat.
But, in fairness, conference time presents
Far worse examples than these pissed-up gents.

Enter **Daisy**.

Daisy (*to* **Denise** *while taking off his coat*)
Bring me a glass of *icy* Chardonnay.

Sees **Farr** *with distaste.*

Then tidy up.

Throws coat over **Farr** *who slumbers on undisturbed.*

The PM's on his way.

Exit **Denise**. *Enter* **Jackson**.

Jackson
I was going to ring you.

Daisy
                    Never mind.
You've never been exactly hard to find.
I came to tell you Tallow's coming round –

Jackson
– In case it's me that's got the middle ground?

Daisy
Now look at these. The latest polls. They show
Conclusively that England's saying no
To more of Tallow, more of you, more Glass,
And saying it so strongly we surpass
The previous record low in their esteem.
It's fortunate we're such a loyal team
Since were disunity to rear its head
The doctors could pronounce this party dead

Denise *enters and puts glass heavily on bar, then exits.*

Daisy
And we could all be working in the press.

Jackson
You're fearful you'll be tainted by the mess?
I bet you've got nowt on beneath that dress.

Embraces **Daisy**.

Daisy
Mmm. Love you too. But Jacksy, this is not –

Jackson *lifts her off her feet and carries her to the settee.*

Jackson
My, Daisy, that's a lovely arse you've got.

Jackson *is clearly intent on intercourse.*

Daisy
We can't do this now. What if Tallow comes?

Jackson
He queues up with the rest.

He turns her round.

But I thought bums
Were more his line and he and Gregor Glass
Were not just chums but avatars of arse.

Daisy (*pushes him back against the bar*)
I don't know why you always want it rough.

While **Jackson** *speaks,* **Daisy** *kisses him, begins to slip off her blouse, unzips his trousers and places her hand inside.*

Jackson
'Cause otherwise I'm never hard enough.
As Farr might say, my sexual excess
Is compensation but it's not success.
It used to be enough to play away
And shag somebody different every day,
But now I have to risk catastrophe –

Daisy
But not here, Jacksy! Somebody might see!

She kisses him again. **Denise** *is seen to the side of stage, watching them on CCTV screen.*

Scene Two

Enter **Glass**. *Comes downstage.*

Glass (*aside*)
Imagine that your only talent is
To plan and execute conspiracies.
Imagine you've not got the slightest sense
Of better times and that the future tense
Is interesting only insofar
As it reveals who your next victims are.
Forget the welfare bill and health and Balkan strife:
Mine is the pure, the politician's life,
And in my world you . . . *you* don't have a say –
I've never been elected, by the way.
My food and fuel and currency is power.
My object? Seeking whom I may devour.
I may not be a lion, but the cat
I am's no whit less dangerous for that.
I am the deadly Edinburgh puss,
And what I ask is: are you one of us?
And in the case of Jackson I say no,
So that's the end of it. He's got to go.
The issue here is not of principle,
But how and when I exercise my will
To put this workie upstart on the skids
With all the other planks and neverdids.
Wind Eddie up and watch the wanker go.
Watch Jackson's intellectual dynamo,
Professor Brammer, use his brainy fist
To solve a problem that does not exist,
Put cash in Eddie's pocket – understand? –
And Jacksy Jackson's bollocks in my hand.
You say there's an election to be lost?
That's not the widest Rubicon I've crossed.
Oh, I'm not proud – I'll dine with anyone,
And they won't find their throats cut till I've gone.

Exit. Blackout.

Scene Three

Lights up on 'office' area. Enter **Elizabeth**, *followed by*
Miranda.

Elizabeth
Why don't you tell me what you've got to say?

Miranda
I've thought about your offer – how you'd pay
The cost of detox?

Elizabeth
          I will. It's up to you.
This is the only way to show I care:
I've made my move, so come and meet me there.

She tries to stroke **Miranda**'s *hair but is angrily shrugged off.*

Pause.

Get straight, or else there's nothing I can do.

Miranda
I need something to live on, you know, *too.*

Elizabeth
Sign in, accept the treatment, then we'll see.

Miranda
The ballpark price for shushing little me?

Elizabeth
See what the future holds, decide what's best.

Miranda (*indicates the room*)
And keep my case on file with all the rest?
There's something wrong with those who love the law
As if it were the thing they're living for –
So much they have to hold it close at night,
Especially if they're liberal and white.
They dress in silk to serve the daylight arts,
But know the anarchy of dirty hearts –
Lock up, then dim the bedside lamp and sweat –

None more so than the virtuous Lilibet,
Concubine of that great absentee –

Elizabeth

You're right.
What is the law? It's something of the night.
We're all corrupt beyond redemption, so,
Since you won't want my tainted help, just go –

Miranda

Forgive me, Mother, for my wicked tongue.
I'm wild and feckless. Worst of all I'm young,
So what the mind's excreting just gets said –
The only way I know I'm still not dead.
But give me one more chance to cop a plea.
How's this? I'll go, but first you let me see
The colour of your money. You agree?

Elizabeth

It's not as simple as you may suppose.
And as for bargains, well, I don't make those.
But, if you've something sensible to say, begin.

Miranda

You ought to know by now you'll never win.
If this comes to a battle of the wills,
I'm twelve floors up with booze and coke and pills,
But mainly, Mother, this girl runs on rage.
Don't interrupt –

Elizabeth

I wish you'd act your age.

Miranda

If I'd been well brought up perhaps I might.
Now listen. I can keep this up all night.
You say you won't –

Elizabeth

can't –

60 Laughter When We're Dead

Miranda
                                    help me any more.
You say if I lay dead outside your door
You'd step straight over me into your life
As liberal lawyer, blameless, childless wife –

Elizabeth
That isn't what I've said.

Miranda
                        Oh, here we go.
You meretricious dried-up so-and-so.

Pause.

OK, let's try to get the details right.
You say . . . I've got to fight the righteous fight
To get off dope and then you will permit
Me access once more to your life, to whit:
One frozen marriage, London flat
And the constituency house, all that –
The world you've long since ceased to share
With Jacksy boy who's fucking never there,
You think I waited all that time
To join this sorry bourgeois pantomime,
Be company for your reduced old age
And help you to erase that dirty page
Where you lay howling on your back
Before you married Big Bad Jack.

Elizabeth
That isn't true.

Miranda
                    OK. I've spun the facts a bit
Because . . . why not? They make you feel like shit.
But what would all your Third World orphans say
If one day I went out to fucking play
And told them how their staunch defender
Used to flash a mean suspender?
And since Jack couldn't give a damn these days

Then meeting me could mean a parting of the ways,
And that would kill you, wouldn't it, Mama?
He's not in love, but by God, you still are.
Imagine. Just imagine if he knew
The things you put your long-lost daughter through.

Elizabeth
Miranda, you will do as you see fit.
I see you hate me. That's the end of it.
So if it gives you pleasure, tell him, then,
That I was young and slept with other men,
And back when dinosaurs still ruled the earth –

Miranda
You gave me for adoption on my birth.

Elizabeth
I had no choice.

Miranda
                    Then why won't you explain?

Elizabeth
You seem to think that only you feel pain,
That other people's reasons must be fake.
What difference do you think that it would make
To know your father's name? You know he's dead.
He didn't love me and he plainly said
He didn't want you. Where is there to go
From here? Good God, what else is there to know?

Miranda
A wise child knows its father. What's his *name*?
This is my life – it's not some bourgeois game!
Or maybe you don't know and he was just
Your one-night stand the night the condom bust?
Or maybe it was Farr, the drunk *poète maudit*?
That might explain addicted little me –
But let's just see what Mr Jackson says
About your exploits in the dear dead days.

Exit **Miranda**. *Blackout.*

Scene Four

Lights up on **Jackson**. *Enter* **Tallow**.

Jackson
What's the matter, Richard? Can't you sleep?
Well, count your Party. They're all fucking sheep.

Tallow
But not you, James. Or else your wool is black.
When you're invisible I watch my back.
Can I assume that . . . problem's been addressed?

Jackson
You can. I never shit in my own nest.

Farr *has been sleeping on the settee. He wakes with a start and walks blindly but swiftly offstage.*

Tallow
Just a minute. Who the hell is that?

Jackson
That's William Farr. Ex-poet. Drunken twat.
He was my oldest friend and we grew up
Imbibing bitter from the selfsame cup,
But William's thirst has proved a mile too deep.

Tallow
Interesting, the company you keep.

Jackson
He's harmless. Plus he's lonely. Plus he's cheap.

Tallow
I take it that you've heard about the polls?

Jackson
Woe to the man for whom the Paxman tolls.
Conference has always been your stage –
Direct from mouth to box and *Mail* front page,
How often now you've kissed Old England's tit,
But Richard, well, alas, you're losing it.

I thought you'd make an impact when you spoke –
Theatrical as ever, Richard, yes, but folk
Outside the Party, folk who have the vote,
Who've learned your moralistic riffs by rote,
Seem less beguiled when you go on crusade
These days. The Christian soldier's overplayed.
The Neds are scared, man, sweating cobs
In case America destroys their jobs.
It's hard to be a three-term government:
Your fund of moral capital's been spent
And then it makes no difference what you say
Concerning general good and frozen pay
If people think that you're the problem now –

Tallow
They must be made to think again somehow.
We've got six weeks. Six weeks to turn it round
Or spend a decade living underground.
We can't allow . . . these people to just *choose*
The other side. We can't just fucking *lose.*

Jackson
Just let me ask you, white man, who's this *we*?
'Cos you're the only cowboy I can see.

Tallow
You cunt. I've come to ask for your support.

Jackson
Cunt yourself. And Jacksy can't be bought.

Tallow
Well, Gregor Glass might beg to disagree.

Jackson
Then let the Glasshole say his piece to me.
Don't you wonder who pays Gregor's tab
With Millbank too skint now to call a cab?
It isn't you, I bet. It isn't me.
But what about those Lords of Industry
That you ennobled, thinking, well, it's free,

And that they would be satisfied to share
A nation they intend to own? Look there.

Tallow
When I see you I see a dinosaur.

Enter **Glass**.

Jackson
Like Kapital, I'm red in tooth and claw.
Here comes the cavalry. Young Gregor Glass.
What brings you here among the working class?

To **Tallow**.

But OK. Look, it's late. I've things to do.
Come the campaign I'll do my bit for you.

Tallow
And afterwards?

Jackson
                    And afterwards we'll see.

Tallow
It's no good, Gregor, I can't stand this crap.

Glass
I understand entirely, old chap.

Tallow (*to* **Jackson**)
I mean, I do, I mean, it makes me sick.
You come on like some kind of maverick
With some great philosophic game to play.
Whose bloody Party *is* this anyway?

Glass
Let me apply my meagre fixer's art
To win us Jacksy's mind, if not his heart.
Go back and rest. Tomorrow will be worse.

Exit **Tallow**.

Jackson
Well, you should know. You drive the bloody hearse.

Pause.
You've had one go tonight.

Glass

Yes, that's correct.
You handled it like one of the elect –
That's *like*, mind, not the kosher thing:
But not bad for a man who would be king.

Jackson
You're so far up yourself you're out of sight.
So what comes next? I haven't got all night.
A Mickey Finn? A nuclear cigar?

Glass
Your downfall will depend on who you are.
You can't blame me for trying, can you, James?
What's life amount to minus fun and games?

Pause.

Can you imagine how it's going to be
If ever – God forbid – that lot get in?
Fortress Britain, toady to the Yanks –

Jackson
But hocked to all the international banks.
South America without bananas,
Fed on fear, Hail Marys and *mañanas* –
It sounds, it sounds . . . familiar enough.
In fact it sounds like Richard Tallow's stuff . . .
'Socialism's what we do in power':

Glass
We like to think we're equal to the hour.

Jackson
That's revolutionary politics.

Glass
It's only revolution if it sticks.
It only sticks if it's assured support,
Unblinking, ironclad sup*port*,

From all of those who know they should
Come to the Party's aid for Britain's good.

Jackson
What tendency do you embody, Glass,
Apart from one that likes it up the ass?
I always knew your brains were up yer crack
But now you think that history's turned back –
So here we stand in bloodstained '89:
Show us your tumbril. I might show you mine.
Don't take the piss – I might be taking notes.

Glass
So. Those who live by them will die by votes?
Perhaps. We never spoke. I never came
To see you. Right?

Jackson
                    Not stopping, Gregor? Shame.
Such an informal seminar's too rare –
We've so much *ideology* to share.
The 'real world', as you call it, won't allow
Much time for theorising now,
Which means, you must agree, that we should seize
The chance to share our last analyses.

Enter **Brammer** *with* **Miranda**. *He's drunk and she's on
something. She shakes him off angrily.*

Brammer
Oh, sorry, boss. I see you've got a guest.

Glass
You like 'em young, eh, Jacksy? I'm impressed:
You've such a lot of energy to burn
You never seem to feel the need for sleep.
But I must go.

Jackson
                    You've promises to keep.

Exit **Glass**. **Jackson** *goes over to* **Brammer** *and grabs him.*

So, are we sorted?

Brammer (*unfazed, walking over to* **Miranda**)
                    Might say that, boss, yes.
Turned out that I could get it done for less,
So in the end a deal was hammered out
In line with your considerable clout.
. . . But then the comedown. When the deed is done
You still don't feel like holstering the gun,
So what does Sister Midnight have in store?
You've had it all. You think there must be more,
More sex, more drink, more violent exercise,
More of the stuff that civil life denies –
And then some way to still the rush of blood,
Or stick it somewhere it might do some good . . .

He grabs **Miranda**, *who yells and shakes him off. He spits on the floor and shrugs.*

Tonight, though, I've been disappointed, James:
Turns out it's you that's down for Double Games.

Jackson
Now *that* was very delicately put.
But Bobby, what would Mrs Brammer say
If she knew half your games were played away?

Brammer
She'd say what's good for her, which would be nowt.
No harm in what she doesn't know about.
And one more little thing, before I go:
Elizabeth keeps *ring*ing. Now you know.

Exit **Brammer**.

Jackson (*aside*)
I do.
Likewise that Bobby's done his work too well,
Which means that Jacksy has to rule in hell.

To **Miranda**.

It's not so much that Bobby Brammer's bad

As that he's never certain when he's had
Enough of anything he can consume:
So if you love your grandma, lock her room
In case he's overcome by appetite.

Miranda
So I'm alone with Jacksy Jackson?

Jackson (*amused*)

                                    Right.
I'm nearly famous. Yes, love. I'm your man.

Miranda
I hope you do it better than he can.
I only went with him to get in here.
The motherfucker stinks of sweat and beer
And though his mouth's as big as Ayers Rock,
The same, alas, is not true of his cock.

She produces and snorts cocaine at the bar. She offers it to **Jackson**,
who shakes his head and indicates his glass. **Miranda** *shrugs.*

So: was there something for the weekend, sir?

Miranda *sits astride* **Jackson**. *He gently removes her.*

Jackson (*alarmed but intrigued*)
Perhaps. But the position I prefer . . .
Is in the Cabinet and not the nick,
So naturally I wonder why you'd pick
A bloke who's old enough to be your dad
When there are newer versions to be had?
How do I know you're not a tabloid plant
Or one of Gregor Glass's sycophants?
I can't just go round screwing girls your age
And end up dickless on the *Sun*'s front page.

Miranda
Look. I don't care who you believe I am.
My name's Miranda. This is not a scam.

She follows **Jackson** *around the stage.*

Consider me a lucky accident
Or someone the absconded gods have sent
To show that while they do prefer believers
Privileges fall on high achievers –
Bankers, demagogues and atheists
Who think that it's for them the world exists –
The players of my late-night indoor games,
Among whose number I would place you, James.
It is my life's ambition to collect

*As **Jackson** makes to walk away, she grabs his hair from behind.*

The scalps, you might say, of the world's elect.

She releases him.

I might let others touch since they employ me,
But – to you I'm free: why not enjoy me?
I'm here because I've seen your photograph –
That moody one, beside the cenotaph,
Remembrance Sunday, year or two ago –
When you stood in for Dick and stole the show
Among the soldiers in the pissing rain?
I broke the video watching that again.

Jackson
I thought I might have voters but not fans.

Miranda
You made the others look like also-rans.

Jackson (*at the bar, cleaning up the cocaine equipment*)
Tonight someone's already had a go
At shafting me – politically – and so

*Using the settee, **Miranda** climbs on to the bar and approaches him along it, pantherlike, on all fours.*

You'll understand my circumspection, pet.
We haven't lost the next election yet,
Which England – or the press – expect to hear
Announced at any moment. Therefore, though

Blows away residue of coke.

Your offer's very flattering, thanks, but no.

Pause.

Who is it you remind me of? No one.
I know you for a moment, then you've gone.
Let's call a cab. Of course, I'm pleased we met.
That's not the kind of schtick I could forget.

Miranda (*jumps down from the bar*)
I think they broke the mould when they made me.
But anyway, I've nowhere else to be.

Pause.

Look, what you want is some way to explain
The process here. Apply the rational brain,
Take thought, and there's no paradox so vexed
It can't be solved. What crap. I'm highly sexed,
And that's enough, and I just want you next.
Can that be found in any Marxist text?

Jackson
I'd have to check.

Miranda
                    The body's a machine
That makes desire. You know what I mean.
Both Beria and Fidel Castro knew
That the regime runs better for a screw,
And that amid the storms of history
You don't refuse that chance to get – for free –
Relief from all that – all that *consciousness*.
You're gagging for it, Jacksy. Just say yes.
Give in and let desire stop the clock
And let me stay at midnight on your cock.

Jackson
Outrageous eloquence meets sex appeal . . .
And though I'm yet to be convinced you're real
It's harder than it should be to resist

Your argument, and I'm not even pissed,
Despite my efforts over several hours.
The night's invested you with special powers
Which you should really bottle up and sell.
But go on, if you want it. What the hell.

Music up – June Christy's big band version of 'Until'. **Miranda**
continues her seduction as a dance, leading **Jackson** *to the bridge*
pillar, making as if to accept his embrace, then slipping under his arm
and leading him offstage.

Exeunt and blackout.

Act Four

Scene One

Enter **Glass**. **Denise** *is behind the bar.*

Glass (*aside*)
'There's not a household but I keep one fee'd',
And this one worked out very cheap indeed.
Denise's views are plain: she hates the rich,
Especially, as she says, 'that Daisy bitch'.
Denise, my friends, shows us what comes to pass
When you half educate the working class.
Give them degrees that no employer wants
And some turn into vengeful little cunts
Whose grasp of Labour's history outgrows
The economic benefits of what they know.
They stand and wait, intending not to *serve*
But see the Daisys get what they deserve –
And in the process catapult to Hell
Whoever happens to be screwing her as well,
In this case our austere Home Secretary,
The Man of Steel, Prime Minister-to-be –
Or so some commentators seem to think.

He approaches the bar. **Denise** *hands him a glass.*

I think my quiet triumph needs a drink.

Enter **Daisy**.

Ms Daisy Gates. It's kind of you to come
So swiftly from your date with our old chum
The Secretary of State for Home Affairs.
I understand that it's to you he bares
His soul, the dark night of his politics.
He must feel like a dog with several dicks.

Daisy
Forgive me, Gregor, if I'm being slow.
There's something you want me to know you know.

You've got that dreadful little poofter's smirk
You wear whenever you've been hard at work
Destroying some poor innocent's career.
But look. It's late. So why'd you want me here?

Glass (*putting an arm round her shoulder, which alarms her a little*)
You know I'd rather have you on my side,
And you in turn would like your gifts applied
To tasks which will ensure that your advance
Up through the ranks does not depend on chance.
But understand: I need a guarantee
That when it matters you still work for me
And don't presume to exercise a choice,
But – with a passion – serve your master's voice.
To which end I have laboured to attain
An . . . item . . . which makes your position plain.

Enter **Denise**. *She hands a package to* **Glass**, *from which he takes out a video cassette.*

In my book nothing beats security.
Dear Daisy, you'll be quite secure with me.
Denise, help Daisy, if you will, to understand
Exactly what I have here in my hand.

Denise
It's her and Jackson shagging fit to bust.

Glass (*moving away to the bar*)
And while they illustrate the sin of lust
Can their identities be plainly seen?

Denise
It's pretty clear who's who up on the screen.
When she's on top you see the rose tattoo.

Glass
Tattoos? Now that's a vulgar thing to do.

Daisy
You little bitch –

Daisy *goes to hit* **Denise**, *who's faster and puts the head on her.*
Daisy *falls. Her nose is bleeding when we eventually see her face.*

Denise
Howay. It wasn't me who sold me arse
Pretending that I served the working class.
Next time you want your Bollinger on ice,
If I'm your waitress, Daisy, smile. Be nice.
I might have had a another copy made.
Be nice, then, Daisy. Yeah – and be afraid!

To **Glass**.

Another one showed up just after her.

Glass *takes* **Denise** *aside.* **Daisy** *sits on the settee.*

Glass
I know. Discover what she has in mind.

Denise
To help a tired Minister unwind,
OK? You won't be needing MI6.

Glass
If she were simply down there turning tricks
I wouldn't ask you, would I now, my dear?
I've got my glass ear to the wall. Come here

Embraces her, turns her around, speaks into her ear.

And briefly I'll expound the theory
That buys the world for darkness and for me.
In this room I've abolished accidents.
Where sex and power fuse and shed their scents
There's not a sniff or atom we can't use
To make whoever we're opposing lose
Their place, their reputation, shirt and wife.
Denise, it's politics, you see. It's life.
Who would not relish the almighty stink,
The waste of pain and rage and printer's ink
Ignited by a peccadillo, pet?
There's more to Mandy than she's shown us yet,

And – waste not want not – put the bitch to use.
And now: adieu, auf Wiedersehen, vamoose.

Exit **Denise**. **Glass** *joins* **Daisy** *on the settee.*

Daisy
If I'd known what an animal you are –

Glass
You'd still have done my bidding in the end.
Poor Daisy Gates. She's weak. She needs a friend.

He helps her to her feet.

I'll be in touch. But now, just disappear.
I've finished with you for the moment, dear.

Daisy *makes as if to speak.* **Glass** *takes her by the chin.*

Glass
Be sensible. Now not another word.
Your ruin's not been cancelled, just deferred.

Exit **Daisy**.

(*Aside*)
Oh, Gregor. Mmm. Is there a bigger kick
Than giving tarts like her my arse to lick?
Except perhaps the deathless gratitude
Of Tallow when he learns that Jackson's screwed.
Now Tallow thinks a knighthood means I'll stay
Onside, but I shall sell him anyway.
I'd eat myself if I was chocolate.
But do excuse me now: affairs of state.
Whoever seeks to be the big I Am
Should heed the ancient truth: *cherchez la femme.*

Exit **Glass**. *Blackout.*

Scene Two

Office area. Lights up on **Elizabeth**. *Enter* **Farr**.

Elizabeth (*affectionately*)
Well, by my watch it's shortly after three.
And you're not quite the one I hoped you'd be.

Farr
The story of my life – be second best,
But useful in the absence of the rest.
The Prufrock of the Labour power elite,
Fed and watered, chucked out in the street,
Discarded, like an inconvenient clause –

Elizabeth
Why is it drunks can never see they're bores?

Farr
I came here with important things to say,
But whisky made me maudlin on the way –
The golden optic on the highest shelf
Has once more made poor Farr forget himself,

Elizabeth (*kissing him on the cheek*)
Poor William. You *are* the worse for wear.

Farr
Cirrhosis, Lizzy.

Elizabeth
                    Don't you even care?

Farr
The way I see it now it's just the breaks.
In other words, I've not got what it takes
To stake a claim – on life, on love, on art.
My masterpiece is how I fall apart,
Regarding which . . . I don't suppose you've got
The makings of a decent late-night tot?

Elizabeth
What *do* you want, apart from more to drink?

Farr
Well, *you*, of course. What else d'you bloody think
Could lead me to behave like such an arse?
Thing is, Lizzy, you, like, you've got class.

Elizabeth
You're very kind. And sweet. But you should leave
And when you've sobered up see if your sleeve
Still wears the heart you're anxious to display.
It may have vanished in the light of day,
And we both know how bitterly you'd regret
The thought that you – in drink – left me upset.
You understand?

Farr
　　　　　　　How do you manage that,
To stay so kind and graceful when some prat
Comes vomiting his failures at your door?

Elizabeth
Let's just say I've seen it all before.
But there are limits, William. Even you
Can tell when I've got other things to do –
I think, like you, I've left my life too late.
I've sacrificed it to the nation state.

Farr
And that's the reason I've come back tonight.

Elizabeth
And that's why you've been getting pissed. Yeah, right.
He could have rung.

Farr
　　　　　　　He could have, but he won't.
And you know why, if you pretend you don't.
I doubt if he remembers where you are.
Just think: you might have married William Farr.
Jack's always on the piss in some hotel,
Some private padded anteroom to Hell
That likes to think it holds the main event

When it's just somewhere wasted time is spent.
There's booze and Brammer and the rest on tap,
That Lenin-in-his-years-of-exile crap
As if next time the tribe of grateful Brits
Will call him in to Araldite the bits
Of worn-out liberal democracy –
A Labour camp set in a silver sea.
He's not the man for you, Elizabeth.
To be with him's become a sort of death,
To see him just continually absent
Himself from all your life together's meant.
We could have had a family too –

Elizabeth
Careful, William. If you go too far
I'll throw you out – no matter who you are.

Farr
You wanted kids – I know you did. But no:
And where on earth did all that wishing go?

She makes to strike him. He grabs her hand.

Oh, marriages are secret, like the grave –

She steps back.

Elizabeth
Yours may be dead, but mine's still mine to save.
It's mine, OK? Whatever you might think.

Farr *looks at her in desperation.*

Elizabeth
Oh, look. I'll find us both a decent drink.
You want to kill yourself, it's up to you –
I'm long past telling people what to do.

Farr
I've no way left to say what must be said.
Let's hope there'll still be laughter when we're dead.

Elizabeth *pours drinks.*

Elizabeth
I know you love me, William. Course I do.
But who could ever make a life with you?
Whatever I might feel for you, I couldn't bear
The way you wear your failure everywhere,
That great black overcoat of grief and booze,
The way you're guaranteed to miss the cues
To happiness or even competence.
You're terrified of ever making sense
Or finding ordinary happiness
In case that might involve you feeling less
Than the extreme you think your art requires.
Death, my darling, that's what you desire.
But since you're here and we're such tender friends
And since this room is where this story ends
I'll tell you something no one's ever heard.
Remember; you must never say a word.
You think Elizabeth is undefiled?
When I went to the States I had a child
And gave her up and went on reading Law.
My scholarship, remember? '84?
The female of the species, William, 's built
To suffer ills and then accept the guilt.
Then I came back, was reconciled with James
And spent my nights remembering her name:
Miranda, my princess, the castaway
In that New World. And still I like to say
Her name at nights, as punishment. My brain
Is full of broken glass, a special pain
Reserved for those who find the choice they made
Incurs a debt that cannot be repaid –
Here, see this photo.

Hands photograph to **Farr**.

                        You might recognise
Her mother's colouring, her father's eyes –
Sufficient for one life, you might suppose,
Or one, at least, whose medium was prose –

Farr

But what about the child? Where is she now?
You hear of people finding out somehow –

Elizabeth

That's history. There'll be no need for that.
She tracked me down. She's been here in this flat
An hour ago –

Farr

But that's amazing, right? It's great –

Elizabeth

Amazing, yes. And twenty years too late.
She hates me, William. She does. She came
To punish me and learn her father's name.
As bright as James himself and me combined,
She took a week when she had set her mind
On finding me.

Farr

But I don't understand –

Elizabeth

At first it wasn't clear what she had planned.
She rang me up a year back. When she said
Her name, it was a message from the dead,
A miracle, a voice I'd never heard but knew
Must be Miranda's, and I thought: let this renew
The world that stopped when I let go her hand.
But love's not on the list of her demands.

Farr

Dear God. You're certain James still doesn't know?

Elizabeth

I would have been, until an hour ago.
Because I wouldn't say her father's name
She thought she'd see my husband all the same
And see what sort of damage that might do.
I think she half suspects the father's you.
I've let her think that I met up with James

Long after all the youthful fun and games.
Forgive me.

Farr
             What, a ghost paternity?
I'm flattered that you'd even think of me.
Elizabeth, we'd better go and see.
They'll let me in. What danger's poetry?

Scene Three

Lights up on **Jackson** *and* **Miranda** *sitting at either end of the
settee. Both are smoking.* **Miranda** *is jumpy with unspent energy.*

Miranda
Not bad.

Jackson
             Not bad? Right. I'm flattered.

Miranda
                                    Don't be.
You learn to look at things objectively.
This works. This doesn't. That's a load of crap.
Objectively, you're just an average chap.
You beat the pants off Brammer, but that's not,
Let's face it, really saying such a lot.
My girlfriend bet the Brits were impotent:
No coconut, but I see what she meant.

Jackson
You fit with all I've heard concerning Yanks –
You want it all and then you don't say thanks –

He stands up.

So if you don't like good old English cock
Fuck off and sell your arse in Little Rock.
Miranda: someone made you up, I think.
You're leaving now, so, darling, drink your drink.

Miranda (*stretching out on the settee*)
See, what you fail to grasp is who's in charge.
If I walk now, that makes me fifty Large
From any paper I might care to choose
To tell about my nights of sex and booze
And whips and crack and rock and roll with you.
Get notes in small denominations, too.
Oh Minister, oh Puritan, oh Man
Who'll stop Britannia going down the pan,
It must be worth some small expenditure
To stop the tabloids talking to your whore.

Jackson (*leans on the end of the settee*)
The problem is, your trick's just out of date.
These days who cares if Ministers of State
Are found out taking pleasure on the side?
The lad works hard. The lad deserves a ride.
As to the drugs, deniability
At times like this is wholly down to me:
And here the public interest dictates
Your black bag deportation to the States.
I'm, as you say, the Minister, in charge
So take a flying fuck for fifty Large.

Enter **Farr**. *At first* **Miranda** *has her back to him.*

Farr
Look, James, Elizabeth's outside, so please
Just *see* her, man. The woman's on her knees.
Get Brammer, get the girlie out the back
Or Glass'll fucking feed you to the pack.
I mean, you've really got to see her now –

Miranda (*turns round*)
Don't tell the Minister what he'll allow –

Farr (*recognising her*)
Oh, Jesus.

Exit **Farr**.

Miranda
Or maybe I'll just put it to your wife.

Jackson
And tell her what? She knows about my life.
She may not like it but she's not the girl
To drop the bomb because I have a whirl.

Enter **Brammer**.

Bobby, what the fuck's gone wrong with Farr?

Brammer (*at a loss*)
Dunno, boss –

Miranda
                You mean: my dad? You're *shocked*. You *are*.

Jackson
I want Elizabeth kept out of here
Until we make this problem disappear.
Turns out we've got a radgie little twat.

Brammer
No worries, boss. You let me deal with that.

Exit **Brammer**.

Miranda
You praise Elizabeth for loyalty:
The sort she showed in giving birth to me?
You didn't know. Why should you? She's your wife.
All this just happened in her other life
My dad and I, we haven't met till now:
I thought he might be more like you somehow,

Jackson (*with the ground steadily dissolving under his feet*)
But when was William ever in the States?

Miranda
He wasn't. We should synchronise our dates.

Jackson
How old are you?

Miranda
                Nineteen. The proper age

To be *your* daughter, too. But that's a page
In your biography that's staying blank:
You've saved your wad for when you have a wank –
You've too much of the old-time vision thing
To leave you time to spend on parenting.
So hello, Stepdad. Maybe you should thank
Your poet friend.

Jackson
        Nineteen.

Miranda
           Nineteen. Correct.
You'll want to reconsider, I expect:
You must admit this sheds a different light
On how things stack up moneywise tonight.

Jackson
You're wrong.

Miranda
        So how'd you figure that?
You'd have to stage a frigging *coup d'etat*
To smother this one. This is really news.
But do go on. I long to hear your views.

Jackson
You're wrong. The bloody dates are wrong. You're wrong.
It can't be William. It's me. You're wrong.

Miranda *laughs hysterically at the situation. He grabs hold of her and starts to shake her.*

Jackson
It can't be William! You're wrong! It's me!
It can't be William. I'm your father! Me!

Miranda *continues to laugh.* **Jackson** *becomes incoherent with rage, horror and pain. Enter* **Elizabeth**, **Farr**, **Brammer** *and* **Daisy**. **Elizabeth** *screaming.*

Elizabeth (*pushing* **Brammer** *aside as he tries to keep her out*)
Get your fucking hands off me!
Miranda, darling, look.

Miranda *produces the switchblade. The others want to get hold of her but fear it.*

Miranda (*to* **Elizabeth**)
You lied to me!

Jackson
I'm your father, me.

Miranda *turns to* **Jackson** *in despair, with her arms outspread. After a long pause,* **Jackson** *approaches, embraces her, taking the switchblade, and stabs her in the chest. She collapses in his arms.* **Elizabeth** *takes* **Miranda** *as she falls, and cradles her in her arms, finding blood on her hand.*

Elizabeth   You've killed her, James. She was *mine*!

Elizabeth *weeps, holding* **Miranda** *in her arms.* **Farr** *in turn holds* **Elizabeth**.

Brammer (*crossing the stage, seeming to embrace* **Jackson**)
Look, boss, we need some kind of public line.
I'll get the car and bring it round the back,
Then me and Heavy'll shift her, use a sack,
And then we'll say there's been . . . an incident . . .
But now it's done and there was no harm meant.
A stalker mebbes. Get them all the time.

Jackson
Bobby, stop this fucking pantomime!

Enter **Glass** *on the upper 'office' area.* **Brammer** *sinks to his knees, still holding on to* **Jackson**.

Glass
It's finished. Minister kills girl while drunk
Is bad enough, but get this: girl's on junk,
Plus dead girl's mother = suspect's wife.
You'll redefine what's meant by doing life.
'The Minister explained that there had now arisen
Reasons he should spend more time . . . in prison.'
And then there's incest, James, the last taboo.
Imagine what the cons'll do to you.

That's politics. A rough old game, my friend,
Best left to the professionals in the end.

Jackson *howls.*

Jackson
Get out of that, as Eric Morecambe said.

Laughs.

Here's what you get for sleeping with the dead.
You never guessed the corpse would not be cold.
It's all your fault, though you were never told
The means by which your nemesis will reach
Into your heart, and, as it kills you, teach
This lesson: call it chance, or call it fate,
But death and failure – these are your estate,
And in return? – a few fine momentary words
Delivered from the scaffold to the birds.

Jackson *cuts his throat and falls.*

Immense blast of searing white light, with camera shutters and flashbulbs snapping and shouted questions from the media wolfpack. Blackout.

Cold Calling

Julia Darling

The stage play *Attachments* was first performed at the Live Theatre, Newcastle-upon-Tyne, on 13 November 2002, as part of a double bill entitled *Double Lives*. The cast was as follows:

Davina   Charlie Hardwick
Bobby   Trevor Fox

Directed by Jeremy Herrin
Designed by Perry John Hudson

The play was subsequently adapted into *Cold Calling* and filmed live in front of an audience at Tyne Tees Television on 16 July 2003, in a co-production between Live Theatre Company and Peter Mitchell Productions. It was broadcast on 5 August, with the same cast:

Davina   Charlie Hardwick
Bobby   Trevor Fox

Produced by Peter Mitchell
Directed by Jeremy Herrin and Max Roberts
Programme consultant Tony Kysh

Editor's Note

This piece started life as a one-act play entitled *Attachments*, presented by Live as part of a double bill entitled *Double Lives*, which also included a short piece by Sean O'Brien, Julia's fellow writer-in-residence, entitled *From the Underworld*.

Cold Calling is a fine example of Julia's ability to fuse superb characterisation, inventive comic situation and dialogue with an intriguing and surprising storyline – qualities that are winning her an ever-increasing audience.

That the play has now been adapted for television and co-produced by Live gives evidence of the company's mission to create work across the dramatic media, encompassing film and television as well as the stage.

Characters

Davina, *a woman in her late thirties. She's an anaesthetist, wears a baggy jumper, and looks generally dishevelled.*

Bobby, *a vacuum cleaner salesman. Thirtyish, with short hair, quite good-looking, but looks uncomfortable in a cheap suit.*

1. INT. KITCHEN DAY.
(This Could Change Your Life)
DAVINA *is in a smart, but untidy, kitchen, making haphazard sandwiches. She uses a large knife to cut them into rough squares. She is crying as she does this. There are piles of these messy sandwiches stacked around her on plates. A stereo on a shelf is playing angry music (Alanis Morrisette) as the credits roll. There's a photograph on the wall of* DAVINA *with a dark-haired man, arm in arm. There is also a poster in a frame of a woman in belly-dancing gear. On the kitchen wall there is a calendar with a photograph of Fred Astaire and Ginger Rogers. A doorbell rings, but* DAVINA *ignores it, and carries on cutting.*

BOBBY *bursts through the door laden with a modern vacuum cleaner, and various pipes and attachments, as* DAVINA *turns with the knife in her hand. They both scream.*

BOBBY: Good morning! Do you have a moment? I assure you that this won't take long, but it could change your life!

DAVINA *turns the music off. They stare at each other in horror.*

2. INT. KITCHEN. DAY.
(Get Out of my House)

DAVINA: Who the hell are you?
BOBBY: Good morning! Do you have a . . . ?
He backs off as DAVINA *threatens him with the knife.*
DAVINA: How did you get in?
BOBBY: I rang, but no one answered . . . the door was open.
DAVINA: That doesn't mean you can just walk in.
BOBBY: You had the music on.
DAVINA: What do you want?
BOBBY: I've got something to show you.
DAVINA: No thanks.
BOBBY: . . . that you'll be very interested in.
DAVINA: . . . I'm not interested in anything.
BOBBY: I think you might be.
DAVINA: I'm not.

BOBBY: Just you wait!

DAVINA: NO!

BOBBY: THE PLATINUM DELUXE!

DAVINA: What?

BOBBY: It's a vacuum cleaner.

DAVINA: A what?

BOBBY: I've got a card, here!

> DAVINA *doesn't read it. She flicks it away with her knife.* BOBBY *talks very fast.*

DAVINA: I don't want it.

BOBBY: How do you know, that you don't want it? You haven't seen it yet.

DAVINA: Get lost.

BOBBY: There's no need to be rude.

DAVINA: I'm being assertive.

BOBBY: Did you do a course?

DAVINA: That's enough!

BOBBY: Perhaps we could make another appointment.

> DAVINA *waves the knife about wildly.*

DAVINA: OUT! OUT! OUT!

BOBBY: All right. Keep your hair on!

DAVINA: You shouldn't walk into women's houses. I'll report you.

BOBBY: I was given your name by a friend.

> *Beat.*

DAVINA: What friend?

BOBBY: Michael.

> DAVINA *looks horrified. She steps back, mouth open, completely taken aback.*

DAVINA: Michael?

BOBBY: I mean Mr Heart. Mr Michael Heart.

> DAVINA *sits down, shocked.*

3. INT. KITCHEN. DAY.

(The Bag of Dust)

DAVINA *sits staring up at* BOBBY, *who is making headway at last. He stands there looking at her, knowing he has some power.*

BOBBY: In fact, I've got something here belonging to your
  friend . . .

DAVINA: My boyfriend.

BOBBY: Oh, I didn't realise.

DAVINA: What have you got belonging to Michael?

BOBBY: Hang on. Can I just put this vacuum somewhere?

> BOBBY *opens his case, looking for something.* DAVINA *stands up,
> brandishes her knife again, coming closer to* BOBBY, *curious to see
> what he has of Michael's. He looks nervously at the knife.*

BOBBY: Um. Could you put that thing down?

> DAVINA *looks at her hand, realising that she is still holding the
> knife.*

DAVINA: I'm not a murderer, you know!

BOBBY: You feel a bit vulnerable, like, when you do the door-
  to-door.

DAVINA: YOU feel vulnerable?

BOBBY: You get some reet nutters, see. Er, not that you're a
  nutter.

> DAVINA *puts the knife down on the table with a sarcastic look.*

DAVINA: Well?

> BOBBY *holds up a plastic bag full of dust*

BOBBY: This!

DAVINA: What is it?

BOBBY: It's the residue that the Platinum Deluxe sucked out
  of Mr Heart's abode.

DAVINA: What are you talking about? Give it to me.

> DAVINA *takes the sealed plastic bag and looks at it with a
> horrified expression.*

DAVINA: That's Michael's dust?

BOBBY: Yup!

DAVINA: Can I smell it?

BOBBY: The bag is sealed, for hygiene purposes.

> DAVINA *pushes the bag down her trousers.*

BOBBY: What are you doing?

DAVINA: I'm in that bag. I spent a lot of time on that carpet.

BOBBY: I'm sure you did!

> BOBBY *thinks about arguing, then changes his mind, making a
> 'she's a right loony' face.*

BOBBY: Please yourself.

DAVINA *sits down, her body curled around the bag in a possessive way.*

4. INT. KITCHEN. DAY.
(Even A Five Year Old Could Do This)
BOBBY *picks up his notebook and starts again.*

BOBBY: Shall I carry on?
DAVINA: Sorry?
BOBBY: No charge or anything . . . Please.
DAVINA: Oh Christ . . .
BOBBY: Ten minutes max.
DAVINA: What are you going to do?
BOBBY: I'll just clean your carpet . . . for nothing! You carry on.
DAVINA: For heaven's sake . . . Hurry up then!
  DAVINA *returns to her chopping board, ignoring* BOBBY *as he clumsily tries to assemble the vacuum cleaner. He is obviously hopeless at his job. She turns.* BOBBY *tries to look efficient.*
BOBBY: It's so easy to assemble, even a five-year-old could do it!
  DAVINA *sees that he can't work out how the lead extension works. In a patronising manner she walks over to the vacuum cleaner and pulls out the vacuum lead, walks over to the plug and pushes it in. The vacuum cleaner roars into action.* BOBBY *switches it off.*
  DAVINA *stands looking at him.*
BOBBY: See, easy!
DAVINA: Get on with it.
  BOBBY *stands with the vacuum cleaner in salesman mode.*
BOBBY: Do you work?
DAVINA: I'm an anaesthetist.
BOBBY: Fancy! An . . . an . . . Did you do a degree?
DAVINA: Er . . . yeah.
BOBBY: Are you having the day off?
DAVINA: Obviously.
BOBBY: Is that how you met Mr Heart? University?
DAVINA: Yes. He was doing history of art.

BOBBY: Bit of art and a bit of science. Nice combination.

    DAVINA *turns away and starts madly chopping up a cucumber.*

DAVINA: Yes.

    BOBBY *glances nervously at his notebook.*

BOBBY: Funny you should mention science and art because that's what the Platinum Deluxe is all about, a blending of superb modern design with an engine that has the power of a racing . . .

    He turns over the page.

BOBBY: Ear . . . I mean car! . . . Hang on a minute! I never even asked you your name. I'm Bobby.

DAVINA: DAVINA!

BOBBY: Right. It's got a seventeen-foot power cord, with an automatic cord rewinder, a dustbag full indicator,

    She turns to face him.

DAVINA: I don't want to know about the RIGGING, do I?

BOBBY: What rigging? It's a vacuum cleaner, not a ship.

DAVINA: Numbers and watts and turbos and kinds of knots! I don't want to know.

    BOBBY *tries to ignore her, continuing weakly.*

BOBBY: . . . . it's got a non-electric air-driven turbo brush that rotates at over two thousand rpm.

DAVINA: How much does it cost?

BOBBY: I do that at the end.

DAVINA: Let's cut to the end then.

    BOBBY *sighs and takes out his notebook and a pen, writing down the price to show* DAVINA.

BOBBY: This is the shop price!

    DAVINA *squints at the price with an expression of horror.*

DAVINA: Are you serious?

BOBBY: This is the factory price.

DAVINA: Ha!

BOBBY: And this is my price! With a free guarantee thrown in.

DAVINA: Two thousand pounds?

BOBBY: It will be the last vacuum cleaner you ever buy. You get a set of attachments as well.

DAVINA: Why would anyone want to spend that much on a vacuum cleaner? You could go on holiday, you could have plastic surgery, not that I want plastic surgery.

BOBBY: You don't need plastic surgery.

DAVINA: I know I don't need plastic surgery!

She sits down with head in hands, fed up with BOBBY, *sandwiches, everything.*

5. INT. KITCHEN. DAY.

(Presentation)

BOBBY *looks at the plates of badly made sandwiches.*

BOBBY: Those sandwiches look bloody awful. You haven't even cut the crusts off.

DAVINA: What do you know about it, NIGELLA?

BOBBY: Presentation is everything.

DAVINA: Is that what they teach you at vacuum cleaner-selling school?

BOBBY: You're very sarcastic.

DAVINA: Two thousand pounds! You must be mental. It's only a pile of plastic. Look at it! It's not even attractive.

BOBBY: I think it's very attractive.

DAVINA: It's ugly.

BOBBY: It isn't! It's shiny and sleek.

DAVINA: Well, you can just go off together and enjoy the rest of the day. Why don't you take the Platinum Deluxe to the cinema?

(*Anne Robinson style.*) Goodbye.

DAVINA *sneers at him.*

BOBBY *pauses, is about to give up, then tries a new tack.*

6. INT. KITCHEN. DAY.

(Dust)

BOBBY *sits down, facing* DAVINA, *and puts on a new, serious voice.*

BOBBY: Do you ever think about dust, DAVINA? About all the bits coming off people every day? Do you ever think about that?

DAVINA: Probably, when I was a twelve.

BOBBY: Like an aura, clouds of DUST, little organisms, and live mites, and tiny fleas and bits of skin, and flecks of people, trailing behind them everywhere they go, leaving traces on everything they touch. Well, the Platinum Deluxe sucks them all up. It cleans around people, so you can see them more clearly.

DAVINA: Don't be silly. You can't see it.

BOBBY: I can. You feel the difference. You can breathe again. It's the absence of crap. Excuse my language, but there's no other word for it. So many people's lives are full of it. They look sort of BLURRED. I get a feeling when I walk into a house, of all the MATTER in the air, and this house, Davina, is CRAWLING.

DAVINA is offended and shocked. She stands up, furious.

DAVINA: Cheeky sod!

But BOBBY has the upper hand. He stands up and walks around the kitchen, circling DAVINA like a hygiene inspector.

BOBBY: How often do you vacuum?

DAVINA: I get Michael to do it about once a week.

BOBBY: Tut tut. ONCE A WEEK? Is that all?

DAVINA: I don't like the noise.

BOBBY: You can hardly hear the Plat Del. It whispers around the rooms, like a deep breath, like a slow marine creature, sucking plankton from the sea.

BOBBY comes up behind DAVINA, whispering in her ear.

DAVINA: Stop doing that! It's creepy.

BOBBY: And all the little mites and creatures . . . if you could turn their volume up they'd be screaming their heads off, knowing the happy multiplying days are over.

DAVINA: Rubbish.

BOBBY: Happy days of squirming and procreating everywhere, on your mattress, inside your pillow, in the forests of your fabrics, because that's what it's like for a mite in this house, like a lovely happy forest. And you an- an- whatever, doctor.

DAVINA: ANAESTHETIST!

BOBBY: Working all day with germy breath . . .

DAVINA: I wash.

BOBBY: Washing! Huh!

DAVINA: How often do you wash?

BOBBY: I don't need to wash. I vacuum with the Plat Del morning and night. I get free use, see. I can hardly bear to think of my former life.

DAVINA: Well, I'm not dead, am I?

BOBBY: A lot of deaths are unexplained: cot deaths; freak things. You got children?

DAVINA: No!

BOBBY: I expect you want children.

DAVINA: Why?

BOBBY: A lot of women your age do.

DAVINA: It's none of your business.

BOBBY: I'd like children.

DAVINA: Good for you.

BOBBY: You'd want to protect them if you did.

DAVINA: We all live with germs and dust. Native Americans don't hoover their bloody wigwams, do they?

BOBBY: Look what happened to them!

DAVINA *looks worried.* BOBBY *is pleased with himself.*

7. INT. KITCHEN. DAY
(Bobby Talks About Michael)
BOBBY *picks up the photograph of Michael.*

BOBBY: Mr Heart was very interested in my display.

DAVINA: He was having you on! He doesn't care about vacuum cleaners.

BOBBY: You'd be surprised! We went through all the attachments.

DAVINA: He was laughing at you.

BOBBY *looks hurt.*

BOBBY: I'd have known if he was laughing at me.

DAVINA: You probably didn't understand his sense of humour. He's very dry.

BOBBY: Oh well, you know him a lot better than I do. I'm just saying, he was interested in the HEALTH aspect.

DAVINA: He smoked!

BOBBY: Perhaps that's why!

> *Beat.* BOBBY *goes back to the vacuum cleaner.*

8. INT. KITCHEN. DAY.

(Carpet Stain Removal)

BOBBY *wheels the vacuum cleaner over to a carpeted section of the kitchen.* DAVINA *watches crossly, but she wants to carry on the discussion about Michael.*

DAVINA: I hate smoking. I told Michael he couldn't smoke in here. You'll have to go out in the backyard, I said. He didn't like that at all. That was the main reason he didn't move in. Him and his fags.

BOBBY: The Plat Del could clear up that argument.

DAVINA: Cheaper to give up smoking.

> BOBBY *holds up a phallic-looking attachment.*

DAVINA: Very gynaecological.

> BOBBY *raises his eyebrows. He picks up a bottle of ketchup and squirts it on to the pale-coloured carpet.*

DAVINA: What are you doing? Stop that!

> BOBBY *grins, picks up some mustard and adds that too. Then he sprinkles sugar on it. He's behaving like a celebrity cook.*

DAVINA: STOP IT! I'll report you!

> *She runs to the telephone but* BOBBY *turns on the vacuum. The following conversation is shouted over the vacuum noise.*

BOBBY: You've tried your old upright but it just makes things worse. It looks like the carpet's had it, but . . .

DAVINA: TURN THAT BASTARD THING OFF!

> *He squirts detergent on to the carpet using the squirter. There's foam everywhere. He vacuums furiously. Then he turns the vacuum off. The stain has disappeared!* BOBBY *bows, as if he's a performer, although he looks a little surprised that it has worked so well.*

BOBBY: Impressed?

DAVINA: Oh, for heaven's sake!

BOBBY: I can't believe that a clever woman like you, an, an

. . . doctor, for God's sake, wants to live like a pig.
That's the last straw for DAVINA. *She comes up close to* BOBBY, *confronting him.*

DAVINA: That's ENOUGH. Look, BOBBY. Listen to me. I don't want anything. I don't want you here, and I don't want the Platinum Deluxe. I want an ordinary, messy life.

BOBBY: So you're not interested?

DAVINA: You've got it, BOBBY! You finally got it! Hoorah!
BOBBY *starts packing up. He looks as if he is finally leaving.*

BOBBY: I'll be off then.
DAVINA *picks up the squirter.*

DAVINA: Don't forget your squirter.

BOBBY: Can I just get you to sign my list?
She signs, wearily.

DAVINA: Off you go then!
BOBBY *reads her signature.*

BOBBY: HA! DAVINA Number! The woman who numbs all pain! My number's up when I see Doctor Number.

DAVINA: Oh very funny! What's your surname?

BOBBY: You'll laugh.

DAVINA: I doubt it. Tell me anyway.

BOBBY: Bottomley.

DAVINA: Ha ha. What a happy note to end on! Bye bye, Bobby Bottomley.

BOBBY: Ha ha, nice to meet you, DAVINA NUMBER. Hope the party goes well.

DAVINA: It's not a bloody party!
They walk through the kitchen door into the hallway.

9. INT. HALLWAY. DAY.
(Who is Feeding the Cat?)
BOBBY *is clattering down the hallway with the vacuum cleaner and his case. It's much darker in the hall, and they are close together in the gloom.*

DAVINA: By the way, when did you see Michael?

BOBBY: About a week ago.

DAVINA: Tell me about it.

BOBBY: I thought you were busy.

DAVINA: I just want to know.

BOBBY: I rang the doorbell. He let me in. I showed him the vacuum. Then I left.

DAVINA: What did you talk about?

BOBBY: Vacuum cleaners, er, smoking, cats. He's got a cat.

DAVINA: It stinks.

BOBBY: Yeah.

> *Beat . . . DAVINA suddenly remembers something with horror.*

DAVINA: Oh God. The cat! Who's feeding the cat?

BOBBY: I expect he is.

DAVINA: He's not there.

> BOBBY *looks anxious, he steps away, but he can't stop asking questions.*

BOBBY: Where is he?

DAVINA: Oh, doesn't matter.

BOBBY: Have you split up or something?

DAVINA: He's DEAD! damn it!

> *Beat.* BOBBY *looks horrified.* DAVINA *runs back towards the kitchen.* BOBBY *follows her.*

10. INT. KITCHEN. DAY.

(Describing Michael's Death)

BOBBY *comes back into the room after* DAVINA. *She's sobbing. He stands there, helpless and embarrassed.*

DAVINA: Michael's dead.

BOBBY: Oh dear.

DAVINA: That's why I'm making sandwiches. That's what you do when people die.

BOBBY: Why didn't you say?

DAVINA: I couldn't get a word in edgeways, with you and your stupid attachments. I mean, here I am chopping up sodding boiled eggs, and the love of my life has been blotted out, and what happens? An inept salesman comes round and tries to sell me a vacuum cleaner, tells me that my house is dirty and that I live like a pig.

BOBBY: I'm sorry, Davina, I'm really, really sorry.

DAVINA: How stupid is that!

BOBBY: I didn't know!

DAVINA: No. Course you didn't.

BOBBY: How did he die?

DAVINA: He just collapsed. An explosion in his brain. It's called an aneurysm.

BOBBY: An . . . an?

DAVINA: It's all right, don't try and say it!

BOBBY: What happened?

DAVINA: I was driving. He was sitting next to me. We were arguing about smoking. He said, 'More people die from car accidents than smoking,' and I said something like, 'Oh, come on, not that old chestnut!' Then he said, 'My head's killing me,' and he sort of fell forward and jerked. I said, 'Stop messing about, Michael, it's not funny. I don't want to have kids with someone who smokes. What kind of example does it set?' And he's just LOLLING, so I push him, and he falls sideways, and there's blood coming out of his EAR.

BOBBY: What did you do?

DAVINA: I jam on the brakes. We're just coming down over the Tyne Bridge. It's teatime, really busy, and I'm feeling his pulse, all the cars behind us hooting and drivers shouting.

BOBBY: Was he dead? Was that it?

DAVINA: Yes. Just like that!

BOBBY *shakes his head, horrified. He looks sympathetically at* DAVINA.

BOBBY: You shouldn't be all alone! Someone should be looking after you. Lucky I called!

DAVINA *slumps into a chair. She picks up a sandwich, offering him one too. They chew in a desultory kind of way.* DAVINA'*s sandwiches are clearly so revolting that* BOBBY *stuffs his in his pocket when she's not looking.*

11. INT. KITCHEN. DAY.
(Ceilings and Belly Dancing)
They sit close together now, BOBBY *in the role of comforter.*

BOBBY: You can't depend on anything, can you?

DAVINA: Everything was planned. He was going to give up smoking. I was going to get pregnant. I even decorated the spare room.

BOBBY: Time is a healer!

DAVINA: I haven't got time. I'm a thirty-eight-year-old anaesthetist.

BOBBY: What's wrong with that?

DAVINA: It's boring. People can't think of anything to say about it. They just say, oooh and your name is Davina Number . . . fancy!

BOBBY: When you feel better, someone might come along.

DAVINA: It takes so long to get to know anyone.

BOBBY: Yeah, it takes a long time to know someone properly. I mean, people aren't what they seem. Look at me . . . I'm more than a vacuum-cleaner salesman.

DAVINA: Oh yes?

BOBBY: I'm an artist. I paint ceilings.

DAVINA: What ceilings?

BOBBY: I paint pictures on ceilings.

DAVINA: Like the Sistine Chapel?

BOBBY: Sunsets, golden skies, cherubim, silver linings and that sort of thing.

DAVINA: Really?

BOBBY: You've probably got all kinds of hidden depths. What do you do in your spare time?

DAVINA: Well . . .

BOBBY: I bet you've got something up your sleeve.

DAVINA: It's just a silly hobby, nothing really. . .

BOBBY: Go on!

DAVINA: Actually, I'm a belly dancer. I'm in a group. We're called the Swinging Navels.

BOBBY: See, I never would have thought of that, looking at you.

DAVINA: I wear a veil and bells and silk scarves, and fake tan.

BOBBY: Fantastic!

DAVINA: Michael used to like it.

BOBBY: Did he?

DAVINA: He used to say, give us a belly roll, and I'd do a little performance for him. He used to join in sometimes.

BOBBY: I can imagine.

DAVINA: It's good for childbearing

> BOBBY *gets up, chucks a plate of sandwiches into a bin, and starts making new ones.*
>
> DAVINA *is close to tears again.*

DAVINA: Develops the abdominal muscles.

BOBBY: Don't think about that now.

> *He helpfully butters bread.*

12. INT. KITCHEN. DAY.
(Realisation)

BOBBY: I'll finish these sandwiches, shall I? Got any tuna?

> DAVINA *picks up the photograph of Michael and looks at it.*

DAVINA: I know you didn't know Michael, but first impressions, what did you think of him?

BOBBY: Pepper? He had a nice smile.

DAVINA: Yes, he did.

BOBBY: Where's the mayonnaise?

> DAVINA *thinks of Michael's flat and what a mess it was.*

DAVINA: Did you like the flat? The decor? (*She's being sarcastic.*)

BOBBY: Aye, canny.

> DAVINA *looks at* BOBBY *suspiciously.*

DAVINA: Which carpet did you do?

BOBBY: The sitting room.

DAVINA: What day was this?

BOBBY: Last Wednesday afternoon.

DAVINA: Ah.

13. INT. KITCHEN. DAY.
(Michael and Bobby)
Pause. DAVINA *processes this information. She looks at the Ginger and Fred calendar on the wall.* DAVINA *suddenly jumps up and looks at* BOBBY *suspiciously.*

DAVINA: No it wasn't. He was with me last Wednesday.
BOBBY: Must have been Thursday.
DAVINA: He died on Thursday.
BOBBY: Tell you the truth, I'm terrible with my memory. It could have been Tuesday.
DAVINA: You never went to the flat, did you?
BOBBY: What are you on about?
DAVINA: The sitting room hasn't got a carpet. You never met him at all, did you?
BOBBY: Course I met him.
DAVINA: So where?
BOBBY: God, where was it?
　　DAVINA *grabs* BOBBY*'s collar and shakes him.*
DAVINA: WHERE DID YOU MEET MICHAEL?

14. INT. KITCHEN. DAY
(I'll Hoover Your Face Off)
Now manic, DAVINA *has* BOBBY *lying on his back on the table. The vacuum cleaner is turned on . . . she is waving the nozzle above his face. He is terrified.*

BOBBY: Get off us!
DAVINA: Why did you lie?
BOBBY: The bag of dust!
　　DAVINA *looks puzzled, then remembers that there's still a bag of dust tucked into her underpants. She lets go of* BOBBY *and pulls the bag out with disgust, holding it as if it's a dead rat.*
DAVINA: It's not Michael's dust?
BOBBY: No. It's just a sample. We all get one when we do the training. It's part of the script.
　　She throws the bag at him.

DAVINA: And you let me believe it was.

BOBBY: I didn't know he was dead, Davina!

She returns and stands over him, with the vacuum sucker in her hand. She's like his torturer now.

DAVINA: Where did you meet Michael, Bobby?

BOBBY: In a little bar.

DAVINA: In a LITTLE bar? Which one?

BOBBY: Raphael's Bar. I did a ceiling in there.

DAVINA: And where is Raphael's Bar?

BOBBY: By the station.

DAVINA: What was Michael doing there?

BOBBY: He must have popped in for a night cap. It's my local so I was just propping up the bar, talking to anyone who came in.

DAVINA: How did this conversation go?

BOBBY: He just asks me for a light, and I start telling him about what I do, about the ceilings, and he says he might be interested.

DAVINA: In a ceiling? Not a vacuum cleaner.

BOBBY: Yeah. I never told him about the Plat Del. He told me all about you though.

DAVINA: What do you mean?

BOBBY: About how much he loved you, and la di da and moving in. And having to give up smoking. He wasn't pleased about that.

DAVINA: Michael talked about our relationship to a stranger in a bar near the station? I find that hard to believe.

BOBBY: Well, he did.

DAVINA: How odd.

BOBBY: It's not odd at all. I've got an open face. People like to confide in me. It works well in the vacuum cleaner business.

Beat. DAVINA *is suspicious.*

DAVINA: You knew Michael, didn't you?

She comes up close again and grabs his neck.

BOBBY: You're stretching my pullover.

DAVINA: Tell me!

BOBBY: What are you doing?

She turns on the Hoover, which roars into action, and pushes him backwards again on to the table.

DAVINA: I'll hoover your face off!

BOBBY: You're a cracker.

She pushes him down, the nozzle in his face

DAVINA: Tell me!

BOBBY: Get off me with that thing. It's lethal.

DAVINA: Can it suck up lies? That would be a useful appliance, wouldn't it? A vacuum that could get the shit out of men.

BOBBY: Help!

DAVINA: TELL ME EVERYTHING!

BOBBY: I WILL. I WILL !

She turns it off, but holds the nozzle to his head like a gun, prodding him.

15. INT. KITCHEN. DAY.

(The Truth)

BOBBY *sits up carefully, with the nozzle to the side of his head.*

DAVINA: Well, Bobby Bottomley?

BOBBY: I knew him.

DAVINA: You met him in this bar?

BOBBY: Yeah.

She prods him.

BOBBY: No, before that.

DAVINA: When?

BOBBY: He visited me in prison.

She's shocked. She lets him go again and walks about, still holding the nozzle.

DAVINA: In prison?

BOBBY: I was in Durham.

DAVINA: What for?

BOBBY: You don't want to know.

DAVINA: What for?

BOBBY: Fraud.

DAVINA: What kind of fraud?

BOBBY: It's quite funny really. I pretended I worked for the

Friends of Siberian Orphans! I went round Jesmond with a collecting box! I was young, and idealistic.

DAVINA: How pathetic!

She sneers at BOBBY.

DAVINA: I knew he did prison visits. I didn't think he met people outside though.

BOBBY: I've known him for years.

DAVINA: Why would he want to meet you?

BOBBY: Why not?

BOBBY *gets up, brushing himself off.* DAVINA *is trying to work it out.*

DAVINA: I've seen that bar, driven past it.

BOBBY: It's just a little place.

DAVINA: What do they call it round there?

BOBBY: I don't know. A street?

DAVINA: It's a gay 'village', isn't it?

BOBBY: Some of it, yeah.

DAVINA: Are you gay?

BOBBY: That's none of your business.

DAVINA *points the vacuum at him again (she's behaving like Sigourney Weaver in* Alien*).*

DAVINA: It's all my business now, BOBBY.

BOBBY: Maybe I am.

DAVINA: I said, are you gay?

BOBBY: Yes. Usually.

DAVINA: Usually?

BOBBY: YES! YES.

DAVINA: So you met Michael in a gay bar, and you'd been meeting him for some time.

BOBBY: On and off.

DAVINA: But you never went to his flat?

BOBBY: No, I didn't know him that well. It wasn't that kind of thing. He wouldn't have invited me round or anything. It was casual.

DAVINA: And Michael never mentioned this to me. Why do you think that was?

BOBBY: How should I know?

DAVINA: But he told you about me?

BOBBY: Coz he loved you and everything. He was mad about

you. It was quite boring actually.

DAVINA: It doesn't fit in with who I thought he was.

BOBBY: Michael Heart. Your boyfriend.

DAVINA: This is just the start of it, isn't it?

BOBBY: You've got to have some secrets in a relationship.

DAVINA: There's more. It's like tugging at a tiny hole in a nylon stocking, and soon it's all hole.

BOBBY: It was only a quiet drink every now and again.

DAVINA: You're lying.

BOBBY: Why would I lie?

DAVINA: Have you got a partner, Bobby?

BOBBY: No.

DAVINA: Why not? You're QUITE nice-looking.

BOBBY: I split up with someone quite recently.

DAVINA: Who was that?

> BOBBY *looks about furtively, seeing the photograph of Fred and Ginger on the calendar.*

BOBBY: Fred.

DAVINA: Fred?

BOBBY: He had ginger hair.

DAVINA: And I suppose he was a good dancer too!

> DAVINA *glances at the calendar.* BOBBY *realises that she knows he's lying.*

BOBBY: I'm sick of you going on at me. It's not my fault he had an an – ?

DAVINA: ANEURYSM! Did you sleep with Michael?

BOBBY: What? Course I didn't.

DAVINA: Just tell me the truth.

> DAVINA *raises the vacuum nozzle again.*

BOBBY: You're being ridiculous now. You're in shock.

DAVINA: You did, didn't you? You were lovers. Look at me, BOBBY. Look me in the eye and deny it.

BOBBY: I never.

DAVINA: You can't look at me, can you?

BOBBY: Oh God.

DAVINA: You did!

BOBBY: YES I DID!

> DAVINA *is appalled. She is on the verge of tears.*

DAVINA: How often?

BOBBY: Put the Hoover down. I can't talk while you're
holding that thing.
She does, slowly.

16. INT. KTCHEN. DAY.
(Hating Michael)
DAVINA *leads* BOBBY *back to the table. She sits him down and hands
him an egg sandwich as if it's a punishment.*

DAVINA: Here. Have a sandwich and sit. Let's hear it from
the top.
BOBBY takes the sandwich and chews it bravely.
BOBBY: I wish I'd never come here.
DAVINA: Why did you come?
BOBBY: To sell you a Plat Del.
DAVINA: I don't think that's why you came.
BOBBY: I haven't done anything wrong, have I?
DAVINA: What do you want exactly?
BOBBY: I don't want anything.
DAVINA: Did you know Michael was dead?
BOBBY: These sandwiches have hardly got any fillings in.
DAVINA: Did you?
BOBBY: YES. YES . . . IT WAS IN THE BLOODY
JOURNAL, STUPID! Everyone knows. You want the
truth, DAVINA? Your life is falling apart. Your dead
partner Michael had a boyfriend, and a whole other
existence out there in the GAY VILLAGE, and he
never said a word about any of it. And instead of
disappearing into his dingy little life, the boyfriend won't
go away. In fact, he's in your HOUSE. Why should you
get all the GRIEVING . . . I WANT SOME!
DAVINA: It can't have been that serious. He was going to
move in with me, for God's sake. He wouldn't even let
you through his front door!
BOBBY: But he spent plenty of time at my house. Couple of
nights a week sometimes when you were working. That
fortnight you were in Birmingham . . . He liked you, but
it was me he fancied.

DAVINA: Stop it!

BOBBY: At least he was honest with me. I knew he had another life. Christ, we talked about you enough. You can't have both, I told him. She'll find out sooner or later. I said he should be open with you, but he said you'd kill him.

DAVINA: The bastard . . . the lying bastard . . .

BOBBY: I told him, but he wouldn't listen.

DAVINA: The bastard cowardy shite.

BOBBY: Do you hate him?

DAVINA: Yes. I do. I really hate him.

BOBBY: I really hate him too. He's left a hell of a mess.

DAVINA: I'll kill him!

BOBBY: Where are you going?

DAVINA: I'm getting him.

> DAVINA *runs out of the door and upstairs.* BOBBY *is alarmed and scared. There are sounds of crashing and dragging something heavy from another room.*

17. INT. KITCHEN. DAY.
(The Ashes)

DAVINA *runs out of the room and comes back with an urn of ashes that she empties on to the floor.*

DAVINA: Have him! Go on, BOBBY. Hoover him up! Take him away! He's all yours.

BOBBY: Is that him?

DAVINA: Get rid of him. Put him in a sealed bag. I don't want to think about him again.

BOBBY: You can't do that.

DAVINA: Oh yes I can. What are you waiting for?

BOBBY: That's Michael. I can't.

> DAVINA *turns the vacuum cleaner on, waving it about in a crazy manner.*

DAVINA: I'll do it then!

BOBBY: No! It's not right!

> BOBBY *struggles to take the vacuum cleaner off her, nearly succeeding.*

DAVINA: GIVE IT TO ME!

> DAVINA *grabs the vacuum back, pushes* BOBBY *out of the way, and starts to suck up the ashes. Then she panics, and changes her mind. The vacuum is roaring away.*

DAVINA: What am I doing?

BOBBY: I told you.

DAVINA: Turn it off!

BOBBY: All right, I'm trying.

DAVINA: I've got to put him back. I didn't mean it.

BOBBY: He's in the bag now.

DAVINA: Get him out again!

> DAVINA *lurches forwards and pushes a switch and Michael's ashes come whooshing back out of the vacuum covering them both. There's dust everywhere. They brush at themselves madly, hysterically. It's a moment of absolute horror. The ashes are sticky and everywhere. bobby turns the vacuum off.* DAVINA *screams, and starts pulling off her clothes. bobby runs to the sink and tries to wash the ashes from his face and neck.*

BOBBY: UGH! He's everywhere. He's all down me neck!

DAVINA: What have I done? Get him off me.

BOBBY: Stop shouting, DAVINA. What did you do that for?

> DAVINA *slumps into a chair, weeping, while* BOBBY *gets a wet cloth and comes up to her, trying to sponge the ashes off her.*

18. INT. KITCHEN. DAY.
(I Shouldn't Have Come)
The chaos has subsided and they stare at the mess.

DAVINA: I loved him.

> BOBBY *kicks the vacuum cleaner.*

BOBBY: Bloody Plat Del. It's fuckin' (flippin') useless.

DAVINA: Look at us!

> *She starts to laugh hysterically . . . then he laughs too . . . but then the laughter subsides.*

DAVINA: I remember him dancing, you know, the belly dancing. He'd get dressed up in my costume, and once –

> DAVINA *picks some grit from her hair and looks at it with horror.*

BOBBY: Go on.

DAVINA: I was watching him standing over there, just where you're standing, rolling his hips, giggling, and I knew it, like a brick in my stomach. He's gay, I thought. But then I thought, does it matter? Does it really matter? He's a nice man. He's kind. He's got a nice smile. And I wanted kids, Bobby. I wanted them really badly.

BOBBY: He should have been open. I would have told you, if I was him.

DAVINA: Yeah, well, it's too late now.

BOBBY: I shouldn't have come.

DAVINA: I could have carried on deluding myself. No, it's better.

BOBBY: Now what?

DAVINA: I'll get back to numbing people. Did you know that anaesthetists are generally fun-loving people? It's because we have to make jokes all the time, to relax the patients before they go under. How many anaesthetists does it take to change a light bulb?

BOBBY: I dunno. How many?

DAVINA: One hundred, ninety-nine, ninety-eight, ninety-seven . . . But no one ever hears the punchlines.

BOBBY: I would.

DAVINA: What?

BOBBY: Listen to the punchlines.

DAVINA: What do you mean?

BOBBY: I could come round again.

DAVINA: What for?

BOBBY: We could get to know each other.

DAVINA: You and me?

BOBBY: I'd be honest with you.

DAVINA: Is that what you're selling? Honesty?

BOBBY: I was thinking, if you still want children, I'm here.

DAVINA: You and me? You're bloody mad! ME and YOU?

BOBBY: Yeah.

DAVINA: Get out, Bobby!

BOBBY: I can't go out like this . . . I'm covered in . . . in . . . corpse.

DAVINA: I suppose you want to use the bathroom now?

BOBBY: I don't mean sex.

DAVINA: What then?

BOBBY: You know.

> DAVINA *picks up the gynacological attachment and looks at it with horror.*

DAVINA: Artificial insemination?

BOBBY: Why not?

DAVINA: It's a bit cold.

BOBBY: You could warm it up in the microwave.

> DAVINA *, still holding the attachment looks at him with horror.*

BOBBY: It was just a thought. (*Beat.*) Sorry.

> BOBBY *picks up the vacuum and leaves.* DAVINA *just watches him go with a shocked look on her face. Just as the credits roll, she realises that she is still holding the attachment.*

DAVINA: BOBBY! Wait! You've left your squirter. Come back!

> *She runs through the door after him. A hint of Turkish music.*

by the authors and published by Methuen

C. P. Taylor
Good
And A Nightingale Sung

Alan Plater
Peggy For You

Lee Hall
Plays 1 & 2

Sean O'Brien
The Birds
Keepers of the Flame